LAST CALL TO SAINTHOOD

Embracing the urgency to ignite
a renewal of faith.

By
Stephen Lawrence

Copyright © 2022 by Vocal Ministries
A Vocal Ministries Publication
Vocal Ministries
Ormond Beach, Florida 32174
www.voicesoflaity.org

Unless otherwise indicated, Biblical references are from the 'NEW AMERICAN STANDARD BIBLE (NASB) ® Copyright © 1960, 1962, 1963, 1968, 1971, 1972, 1973, 1975, 1977, 1995 by The Lockman Foundation. Used by Permission.

All rights reserved. No part of this publication may be reproduced, distributed or transmitted in any form or by any means, including photocopying, recording, or other electronic or mechanical methods, without the prior written permission of the publisher, except in the case of brief quotations embodied in critical reviews and certain other non-commercial uses permitted by copyright law.

Last Call To Sainthood / Stephen Lawrence
ISBN: 978-8-9867324-0-4

DEDICATION

To my family, friends, and ministers of God's Word, that played a critical role in supporting me though my life's faith journey. I appreciate you and pray that you may continue to be blessed with God's amazing grace.

CONTENTS

PART ONE A CALL TO HOLINESS 1
FORMULATING A PLAN FOR RENEWAL 1
THE WORLD CONDITION 9
AN EXAMINATION OF CONSCIENCE AND FAITH 13
WHAT IS SIN? 21
DREAD THE LOSS OF HEAVEN, PAINS OF HELL 29
LISTENING TO GOD 41
THE BIBLE 49
MISSIONARIES FOR CHRIST 61
THE HYBRID CATHOLIC 67
LOVE, LOVE, LOVE 71
PART ONE CONCLUSION 75
PART TWO LOST KEYS TO THE KINGDOM 77
WHO LEFT THE DOOR UNLOCKED? 79
SEXUAL SIN, THE CHURCH AND REPENTANCE 85
PART TWO CONCLUSION 97
PART THREE THOUGHTS AND PRAYERS 99
THE SACRAMENTS 101
THE BLESSED VIRGIN MARY 109
PURGATORY 115
ABORTION 119
SEXUAL SIN 122
DIVORCE 125
TITHING 127
SALVATION BY FAITH 131
AMEN! 134
BIBLIOGRAPHY 137

"I pray that the eyes of your heart may be enlightened, so that you will know what is the hope of His calling, what are the riches of the glory of His inheritance in the saints, and what is the surpassing greatness of His power toward us who believe."
(Ephesians 1:18-19)

PART ONE
A CALL TO HOLINESS

I

FORMULATING A PLAN FOR RENEWAL

Do not be conformed to this world, but be transformed by the renewal of your mind, that by testing you may discern what is the will of God, what is good and acceptable and perfect.
Romans 12:2

Greetings to all my Catholic/Christian brothers and sisters. May grace from God Our Father, the peace and joy of the risen Jesus Christ, and the gifts sent forth by the Holy Spirit be with all of you. Let us be thankful together that God has chosen us to become His children, members of His Bride, the Church.

As conscientious followers of Our Lord Jesus Christ, one of the most important callings we have is to actively share the 'Good News' of the gospel. I hope that the substance and content depicted on these pages will offer an elevated source of inspiration to its readers. Our goal is to open hearts and minds to the urgency of the challenges God has set before us. These turbulent times in our history dictate addressing the crucial needs facing Christian laity. Especially the need to make a sincere commitment to rededicating ourselves to the acceptance and evangelization of God's Word and His message of salvation.

Lacking a renewed sense of devotion to these objectives, we risk suffering the loss of a great number of Catholic/Christian souls to the influences of today's world. There needs to be a restored awareness focused on the powers of the Devil, God's ultimate judgment, and the often neglected prospects of eternal torment. The time has come to 'awake from our slumber.' Let us find the God-given power within us to grasp the fire of the Holy Spirit absent from so many of our parishes and congregations today.

Many Catholics, particularly in the US and Europe, have abandoned the Church over the last 30-40 years. In fact, we could probably count this group as one of the largest Christian denominations in the world today. We might also speculate that a good percentage of this cohort has become spiritually 'neutralized.' They no longer feel the need to pursue further, or even maintain the existing level of their personal relationship with God.

Adoption of these apathetic attitudes leads to ignoring the eternal consequences associated with them. Many put their hope in a commonly accepted satanic deception that 'everyone goes to Heaven.' Recently, this mindset has trickled down from the very highest levels of the Vatican to our parish pulpits.

Judgement, Hell, and eternal torment are now considered obsolete, nonexistent concepts. Some will say they only exist for the very worst of humankind. For those with faith now grown dormant, a stark reawakening to the truth is required. A sincere renewal of devotion will be necessary to bring their souls back to a more vibrant spiritual life, rekindled in pursuing salvation.

It is easy to identify so many in the Catholic/Christian community that have adopted these 'lukewarm' spiritual convictions. As a result, Satan has seized this opportunity to ramp up his attacks on the Church and capture greater dominance over today's world populations.

I FORMULATING A PLAN FOR RENEWAL

The ongoing crisis and calamities plaguing the Catholic Church and its leadership are well documented. Online articles and literary works in the marketplace provide us with endless details on these subjects. These documented self-inflicted wounds, and the implications carried over to the laity, are not exclusive to the Catholic faith. They affect many other Christian denominations as well.

This book touches on some of these concerning issues to give relative cognizance to readers. However, it is not the primary intention of *'Last Call to Sainthood'* to expand on these topics. Rather, this book was written to deliver a simple, practical, straightforward message and plan to help support and rebuild the faith and devotion of Catholic/Christian laity.

Our goals are to help inspire an awareness to not only reconsider the levels of our individual connections and devotion to God, but also to embrace one of God's greatest commands. Evangelizing others to do the same. The spiritual welfare of the laity is increasingly in danger of being compromised by the diminished effectiveness of the clergy. As a result, we must now make it a priority to come together in one voice as laity, encouraging and supporting one another.

To supplement the contents of this book, we created an associated website, Voices of Catholic Laity (VOCAL) Ministries, www.voicesoflaity.org. We dedicate our online lay ministry to providing information and multiple resources to enhance your faith journey. We also provide opportunities to share your own stories, testimony, and ideas.

To be sure, there are different perspectives for defining 'Sainthood.' As Catholics, we often look only at those men and women recognized by canonization in the Church as true saints. But as St. Paul tells us multiple times in his Epistles, we are all called by God to strive to become 'saints,' (Rom 1:7; Eph 1:1: Eph 1:18-19; Eph 4:12; Phl 4:21; Col 1:1). In these related passages, St. Paul identifies those in the early Church who have become believers and followers of Christ and **endured in their faith** as 'saints.' We too can heed God's call to sainthood by taking the steps necessary in consecrating ourselves to becoming loyal followers and servants of Jesus. Living through example, our mission is to spread the 'Good News' gospel of salvation through our faith in His life, suffering, death, and resurrection.

Thousands of godly saints are alive today and a great number have gone before us. The overwhelming majority of these Christian martyrs and saints you will have never heard of. Their life stories are obscure to us, but so present and influential in the lives and eternal destinies of those they touched with God's grace. My heartfelt hope is that you will join me in seeking a pathway to sainthood, on what could be part of the last crusade to enlighten the hearts and souls of the Catholic/Christian faithful with God's wisdom and graces.

Offering you no credentials as an 'expert' on Catholicism or Christianity, I'll quote St. Paul in his first message to the Corinthians: 'I humble myself before you in weakness, trembling, and fear (1 Cor 2:1-5).' Lacking the qualifications of a well-known best-selling author or high-ranking member of the clergy, instead I reach out to you with a sincere heart as a fellow lay Catholic/Christian. Grounded in the Word of God and inspired by the Holy Spirit, I hope to offer support and guidance to those ready and willing to enhance their relationship with God and follow a path toward holiness and sainthood.

Observing the human condition around the globe, it is easy to identify the high level of influence evil has gained over the past several decades. We should give careful consideration to the possibility that God's judgement and the end of this age may soon be upon us.

As Catholics and Christians, do we stand vigilant and ready for the persecution of our people and faith to intensify? Is it possible to endure in our faith with little or no support from our bishops or the Church in Rome?

Right now, in this moment and place, the time has come to adopt a sense of urgency in summoning the Holy Spirit to deliver us His gifts of wisdom, fortitude, and courage that will be so essential if we are to survive this impending spiritual oppression. A new age of martyrdom is imminent and will

I FORMULATING A PLAN FOR RENEWAL

gradually present itself to those remaining few who can endure in the faith. We must stand firm as the 'deep state' and the 'deep church' collaborate to slowly bring 'One World Religion' and the 'New World Order' into power.

Do not be anxious, angry, or fearful as you come to witness the gradual falling into place of the new political and religious systems that will come to rule our world. We can even expect that the leadership of our Roman Catholic Church will be complicit in this transformation.

Know these things have been prophesied in the Scriptures (Rev 13:1-18) and must come to pass before Our Lord's return and God's final judgement on humanity. The Gospels tell us the disciples of Jesus were riddled in disbelief and despair when He told them He must go to Jerusalem to suffer and die at the hands of the Jewish leaders but will rise after three days (Matt 16:21-23; Mark 10: 32-34). So, we too should take warning of the looming tribulations (Acts 14:22; 2 Thes 2:3), while maintaining our hope in the promise of the second coming of Christ.

The content of *'Last Call to Sainthood'* is divided into three parts.

Part One 'A Call to Holiness' outlines different areas and steps I believe can help guide us into a state of spiritual rediscovery and a closer personal relationship with God. These are, from my point of view, critical stages and concepts we can follow toward aligning our spirit with God's will, encouraging others, and receiving the motivation necessary to share the true Gospel of Jesus Christ with as many people as we can.

Part Two 'Lost Keys to the Kingdom' stresses the reasons behind why it is so important for us, as laity, to take immediate actions. Reflecting on the immorality and apostasy that has penetrated all levels of Church hierarchy over the last several decades, we analyze the existence of the spiritual chasm created between the clergy and the laity. Searching for ways to work toward filling this void, this section encourages us to recognize the reasons we can no longer put our full trust in Church leadership. Absent of confidence in Church governance, we need to find the means to inspire our own commitments to pray, work, and worship together by evangelizing the good news of the gospel. The ultimate 'end-game' should always be the redemption of our fellow Catholic/Christian brothers and sisters (Prov 24:10-12).

Part Three 'Thoughts and Prayers' offers some of my viewpoints/comments on a wide range of Catholic doctrines and relevant modern-day topics.

Using this platform as a tool to express my religious philosophies, views, and experiences, I can't and don't pretend to know I'm right in all my beliefs and trust only God to be the judge of that. Some values I hold dear are, from my perspective, undisputable. While for others, I still pray for answers. It would not surprise me to learn that this might hold true for many of you as well.

My aim is not to convince you I, or even the Catholic Church, have the absolute right path to follow to ensure one's redemption and salvation. Instead, I will share critical lessons I've learned from both inside and outside the teachings of the Catholic Church that have brought me to a more intimate relationship with God and a better understanding of His Word. My hopes and prayers are that sharing these experiences will help lead you in that direction as well.

Identified on the following pages are fundamental biblical truths and philosophies, some of which I believe have eluded so many Catholics/Christians in their lifelong course of worship. Not necessarily through their fault, but because these fundamental spiritual ideas and attitudes are not delivered to us regularly by parish clergy.

Growing up in the Catholic faith there is no doubt in my mind I would have missed out on so many of God's spiritual gifts and blessings had it not been for keeping an open mind and heart to the teachings of Godly men and women from outside of Roman Catholicism. Our ultimate goal in life has to be identifying God's grand plan for each of us, and I hope that by sharing my words and ideas, we can embark on this journey together in God's Holy Spirit.

I FORMULATING A PLAN FOR RENEWAL

So whether you are like me in your 'twilight' years, in your twenties, thirties, or wherever you are in both your life and spiritual journeys, I am optimistic that the following pages will serve as a spark to rekindle within you a deeper devotion to God.

I would strongly suggest having a Bible close by your side as you read through this book. As you may have already noticed, there are many biblical verses referenced in each of the chapters that are very relevant to the content and the message.

I look forward to continuing the relationship with readers by having an ongoing dialogue that includes sharing views on the philosophies presented in this book, hoping to generate some great discussions that will inspire all of us. Please visit our website and blog at to access great resources and take part in some of the ongoing dialogues and conversations.

www.voicesoflaity.org/blog

II

THE WORLD CONDITION

You adulteresses! Do you not know that friendship with the world is hostility toward God? Therefore, whoever wishes to be a friend of the world makes himself an enemy of God.
James 4:4

A shrewd decipherer of end-time events foretold in God's Word can relate to the global acceptance of many worldly doctrines since the 1950s. The tolerance of these ungodly principles gives rise to certain questions, as our society continues to turn further away from God every day. Is this the beginning of His judgment on the United States and the world? Is His judgment on the Holy Catholic Church coming to a climax given the apostasy existing at the highest levels of its leadership? Is the 'New World Order' prophesied in Revelations (Rev 13:1-18) coming to pass?

When I started writing *'Last Call to Sainthood'* in the fall of 2018, things were going pretty well in this country (US) and the world. We could not say the same for the Catholic Church.

Feeling some sense of urgency to proclaim the message that was inspired in me, never did I expect things would deteriorate so quickly. Never would I have guessed the birth pangs of God's judgment would manifest themselves in such a short time.

Since I began writing this book, so much has happened. The worldwide COVID-19 pandemic has infected and killed millions of people around the world. God truly has humbled us, showing just how vulnerable we are as a society. This virus in two years has raised havoc on our economic, political, social, educational, and health care systems. It has pushed us into bankruptcies, quarantines, states of loneliness, depression, and gripped people across the globe with related fears and anxieties, diminishing the psychological and spiritual well-being of so many. To make things even worse, church services in many parts of the country and the world have been all but canceled, restricting our ability to worship together.

Besides the outbreak of the pandemic, there have been many attacks on so many of the foundations of our society. During the summer of 2020, several major US cities were literally and figuratively burning. Demands are being made and supported by certain groups and politicians to tear down police forces threatening our very safety. Police officers are being blatantly and brutally attacked by angry mobs, with no consequences to their actions. Rioting, looting, and destruction of personal property have become the norm, including the recent chaos in the Capitol Building in Washington, DC.

A growing percentage of younger adults in our nation are being compromised and indoctrinated at many levels of our educational systems. Godless doctrines conforming to the viewpoints of educational hierarchy and professors with single-minded agendas are being preached at our nation's educational institutions. Freedom of speech at colleges and universities for anyone with opposing conservative views has been all but taken away.

'Cancel culture' and giant social media censorship have become overwhelmingly prevalent in recent days. The traditional family unit is being assaulted by members of radical organizations. Things have even sunken to the level of malicious damage to religious statues and the intentional burning of Catholic churches both here in the US and around the world. Sadly enough, this is likely just a 'preview of coming attractions.' Pointing us to the desperate need for the laity to organize and become so much more involved in delivering God's genuine message to the world while there is still time.

Certainly not immune from 'attacks,' we can also look at what has happened to the Catholic Church and its leadership. Evidence shows over the past several decades it has been gradually infiltrated and influenced from within its own ranks. These intrusions are the results of schemes devised as far back as 100+ years ago. Slowly the influence of the Communists, the gay agenda, and the Freemasons have penetrated to the highest levels of Church leadership. Some may perceive this as outlandish, but for me, it is not out of the question that Satan has overtaken the very throne of Rome.

A few books I strongly recommend provide great detail on the history and successes of the above-mentioned schemes to infiltrate our Church. The first is appropriately titled *'Infiltration–The Plot to Destroy the Church from Within' by Dr. Taylor Marshall* (Marshall, 2019). Another is *'The St. Gallen Mafia by Julia Meloni'* (Meloni, 2021) that describes 'behind the scenes' plots schemed by a certain clan of liberal minded cardinals and bishops to bring our current Vicar, Pope Francis, to power.

What is concerning to me is the belief that what we are seeing now is just the beginning of a trend that will probably get so much worse as humankind moves even further away from God. It is difficult to identify any signs of sincere spirits of repentance, reconciliation, or remorse coming from the Church to the forefront soon. The more likely scenario is that we will continue to see an increasingly prideful society looking to expand their rights and conforming to 'freedoms' that oppose God's laws. This will come to pass simultaneously as the freedoms for God-fearing citizens continue to be trampled on.

God is loving and patient with us, but there comes a point where He must exercise His judgment to get our attention and convict us of our disobedience. While it may not always seem that way, God's judgment and wrath are not poured out **primarily to punish us.** Instead, it is a demonstration of His love for us, wanting us all to acknowledge our sins and come to Him in repentance. Finding precedent in the Bible, it is easy to envision a paradigm of God's present judgment with the destruction of Jerusalem in 586 BC, foretold by the Old Testament prophets (Isaiah, Jeremiah, Ezekiel, etc). There will be an additional focus on this topic later in Part II.

The realization of God's judgment on the Catholic Church in recent times is easy to discern. Unlike its freedom to do so in the past, the advent of social media has restricted the Church's ability to operate in secrecy. Particularly over the last two decades, we have observed the exposure of a spiraling decay in the moral ethics and values of the Church's clergy and leadership.

Accompanying this deterioration has been a simultaneous decline in engagement by the Roman Catholic laity. Enrollments of qualified young men into our seminaries, the numbers of baptisms, confirmations, marriages, and family attendance at Mass are all examples of Church institutions experiencing rapidly declining levels. I can't imagine how the Church will sustain itself in the future.

We also must express concern for those that are part of the faithful and attend Mass regularly. Are they given the lessons and knowledge necessary for understanding the total embodiment of God's Holy Word and the genuine message of salvation? Are they like I was for so many years, spiritual robots, habitual in their worship, just following along in traditions? How many Catholics/Christians can say that they are aware of **what God's plan is for them** through their prayers and personal relationship with Him? Let's see if we can work together towards a strategy that will assist us in creating an awareness to recognize and fulfill God's intended plan for each of us.

III

AN EXAMINATION OF CONSCIENCE AND FAITH

Test yourselves to see if you are in the faith; examine yourselves! Or do you not recognize this about yourselves that Jesus is in you—unless indeed you fail the test?
2 Corinthians 13:5

A logical but difficult first step in forging a path to sainthood is to take some time to review our life priorities. We need to identify our transgressions against God and evaluate where we are in our relationship with Him through an examination of conscience. I've recently heard this process referred to as an "illumination of conscience," which may in fact be more appropriate.

Beginning this chapter and section with some reminiscing on attending (or not attending) Sunday Mass seemed fitting. I identified my absence from attending Mass/Sunday Service as an obvious sin while making an examination of my conscience several years back. The story below was one that came to the front of my mind. This episode, that goes all the way back to the early 1960s, really illustrated to me how ingrained the Catholic faith had become in my spirit.

Halfway through the morning session of our fourth-grade Catholic school class, they instructed us to line up along the edge of the blackboard on the right side of the classroom. Immediately we got up from our desks and arranged ourselves in alphabetical order, the standard protocol in those days. It was a beautiful, sunny Monday morning in April 1961, a few weeks after Easter. At the front of the classroom stood our teacher, Sr. Mary Francis, and the school principal, Mother Superior, Sr. Mary Hector. They called students one at a time from the 'lineup' to sit in a chair that was positioned between the two of them. Sr. Mary Hector, short and stocky in stature, projected a dominating demeanor. She could intimidate any nine-year-old into telling the truth. She whispered something in each student's ear and awaited their response, which was whispered back. They then posed a second question to each student. Most of those questioned before me went back to their desks. They directed a few to remain standing in the front of the classroom. As my turn approached, I felt a knot in my stomach, and nervously approached the two Sisters.

"What Mass did you go to on Sunday and who said the Mass?" Sister Mary Hector whispered.

"I served at the ten o'clock Mass, Mother Superior," I whispered back.

I never got the second question and was sent back to my desk. Later, I found out from a classmate the second question was 'What was the sermon about?'

When it was over, six of my classmates did not survive the 'inquisition' and were marched over to the adjoining church accompanied by Mother Superior. A priest was there waiting to hear confessions. This public display of embarrassment, and to some extent humiliation, would not be tolerated

III AN EXAMINATION OF CONSCIENCE AND FAITH

at most places in today's world. Back then, it proved to be an effective deterrent to us Catholic school kids for skipping Mass. Reminded of a theme from an old Monty Python skit: You never knew when the next 'inquisition' would be coming.

Leaving behind all worldly claims and devoting their entire lives to serving God and others, nuns never seemed to get the recognition they truly deserved and often ridiculed for their practices. Their dedication to educating Catholic youth was unmatched. They were legitimately concerned with the spiritual welfare of the students under their watch. It was the nuns that taught and made us memorize the Baltimore Catechism, prepared us for the sacraments, and embedded deeply rooted Catholic traditions into our hearts and minds.

While examining my present spiritual condition, I recalled this incident from my youth. Then I asked myself: 'Have I distanced myself that much from God that I can't give Him one hour a week to be with other parishioners praying and worshipping together? Isn't there benefit to listening to God's Word, and taking part in the Eucharist? Is there no better way to give glory and honor to Him, minister to others, and provide financial support to our parish?'

Understandably, a common perception in our current society is that the Mass is boring. Add to this a lack of spiritually compelling sermons being preached by the clergy and sometimes it makes it difficult to argue against this assessment. But what if we could instead embrace attending Mass/Sunday Service with a positive spiritual attitude and realize the great blessings God offers to us each time we attend? It can be such a rewarding experience. From an 'illumination of conscience' perspective, it is not so much that 'missing' Mass or Sunday Service is a grave sin, but it is more to the notion that we do not feel the need to honor or love God enough to spend time with Him on His anointed holy day.

Here's an interesting quote I found regarding the Mass from Pope Francis in February 2014: "If you do not feel in need of God's mercy, if you do not feel you are a sinner, then it's better not to go to Mass, because we go to Mass because we are sinners and we want to receive the forgiveness of Jesus, to participate in His redemption, His forgiveness..."–2/12/14.

Like with any human personal relationship, our connection with God can waiver as we go through different phases of our lives. It is critical for us to frequently take a step back and evaluate the true level of our devotion and obedience to God through a complete examination of our conscience. **Being in a constant state of discernment and repentance is a crucial first step in bringing us closer to God and sainthood.** Sincere repentance is a key trigger in the transformation of our hearts, minds, and souls to God. Mark tells us in his Gospel that Jesus in his very first preaching in Galilee, after John the Baptist was taken into custody, made it a point to reinforce John's call to 'repent and believe in the gospel' (Mark 1:15)

Discernment can prove to be an arduous process as we inwardly search below the surface of our souls to identify the sins in our lives. It is far too easy (especially in today's world) for us to embrace the sinful habits and behaviors we have developed, and view them as being consistent with God's will. The easy road to follow is to make excuses to justify our sins rather than repent from them. How much simpler for all of us would the path to repentance and salvation be if we could identify our sins as easily as we recognize the sins in others?

We reason that if the global masses think something is OK, then surely God must also be on board. This modern day logic is quite contradictory to the Word of God and teachings of Jesus.

The road to salvation made pretty clear to us back in Catholic grammar school, was stated simply. Your soul was like a spotless, clean, white cloth. If you committed a mortal sin, the white cloth would turn completely black. Failing to go to confession, repent, do penance and have God and the Priest remove our mortal sin would cause eternal damnation to Hell. In those days there was no holding back on making it known that eternal torment was in store for those that died in mortal sin and something to be feared.

III AN EXAMINATION OF CONSCIENCE AND FAITH

Venial sins were not as bad. They only 'spotted' the cloth (your soul) with the size of these spots dependent on how 'bad' the venial sin was. If we did not remove these sins through confession before death, you ended up in Purgatory.

They taught Purgatory to be a place of temporal punishment to purge and cleanse your soul until God deemed it acceptable to go into Heaven. The longevity of your sentence in Purgatory would depend on the extent of the seriousness of your unforgiven venial sins and could be hundreds or even thousands of years. You could, however, redeem a 'get out of jail free' card from Purgatory through a plenary indulgence. You earned these indulgences through prayers and/or sacrifice before death, or from someone still living on earth after you die through intercession. To go directly to Heaven after death, you had to die in a 'state of grace' with a completely white soul.

To anyone reading this born after the mid-1960s, these beliefs and attitudes may sound completely absurd, but it was a very real teaching of the Church. To their credit, if you look closely, the Church has 'officially' not veered very far from its position regarding these standards, but **most times preaches quite the opposite**.

As I look around the sparsely populated pews at Sunday Mass, I think about the large percentage of baptized Catholics and other Christians that do not give a second thought to attending weekly Mass or church services. This holds true especially for those in the 18-40-year-old category. Certainly not immune to this attitude, I can empathize, being found in this same boat for years at a time during certain stages in my life. In the renewal of my relationship with God, it brings me great joy that through God's grace, I have been able to repent and attend Mass/Service joyfully and faithfully.

It's important to realize that a thorough examination of conscience requires us to take a full look at our lives in terms of both 'what we've done and what we have failed to do.' Surely many of you have dealt with, and perhaps continue to deal with, more egregious sins than missing Mass. In my own experiences, I have endured the pain and suffering that comes with living a life of sin and separation from God. For anyone in that situation now, it is vital they know there is always hope for personal peace through repentance, saving faith in Jesus, and God's redemptive graces. The keys are to identify and acknowledge your sins, repent from them, and then prepare to indulge yourself in God's mercy and blessings.

One of the key and probably most difficult phases of our discernment process is to consider the many things that have changed in our society over the last 50-60 years, and how do we distinguish what is indeed a sin and what is not? What will God truly hold us accountable for?

Fortunately, or some might say, unfortunately, as a young adult, I lived through the cultural 'revolutions' of the late 1960s and 1970s. They continue to have an enormous impact on present-day lifestyles and the choices we make. There's no denying that during these tumultuous times, as I was in my teens and early to mid-twenties, I fully embraced the rebellion against the status quo of society, counted among the front-line foot soldiers leading the charge. Peace, Love, Equality, 'if it feels good do it,' and 'love the one you're with,' were common mantras proclaimed by our 'hippie' generation. Make no mistake, we fought hard against the establishment to win our battles. Protests, boycotts, the dramatically changing music and media scenes, and the availability of a new array of drugs to detach your mind from reality were all part of the new culture. All of this made for a volatile combination that precipitated monumental change, some for the good, and some not.

From a spiritual perspective, the counterculture challenged the norms of accountability and behavior that existed in the Church for centuries. Attitudes toward sin, and sexual sin in particular, completely turned around. It was all about 'freedom.' Freedom with no responsibility or consequence attached to it. It was the starting point of our culture removing the sacredness from sexuality. We took it out of the institution of marriage and dispersed it freely to the masses. Like mini-gods applying our unique standards and rules of behavior, we displayed an almost total disregard and contempt for existing 'old fashioned' moral values defined and defended by the Church back then.

On the other side of the coin, we must also consider some big positives that came from the 'Hippie Movement.' Probably the greatest forward societal strides made during that era were for the civil and human rights of minorities and women. While it is easy to see from current events that our country still has a way to go in these areas, the events of the 1960s and early '70s played a tremendous role in building a great foundation for social progress and justice.

IV

WHAT IS SIN?

For I know my transgressions and my sin is before me. Against You, You only, I have sinned and done evil in Your sight, so that You are justified when You speak, and blameless when You judge.
—Psalms 51:3-4

In Chapter 1, we discussed how making a sincere examination of conscience in today's world is a formidable task, but also an important first step in rekindling and maintaining our relationship with God. Toward the end of the chapter, we considered how much society has changed over the past sixty years. It explains the struggles in our attempts to discern if the sins of the past are just that, or do they still apply? Has God readjusted his standards and values as our society has become more 'sophisticated' over the past sixty years? Is attendance at Sunday Mass/Service still required? What is God's will toward the key moral challenges facing today's society? Abortion, extramarital sex, divorce, and homosexuality are all topics that weren't even considered 'on the table' for discussion in the early 1960s. Is God still looking at these as sins? We all have positions regarding these subjects, but it is so important for us to know that **our eternal destiny hinges on our efforts and ability to recognize and understand God's true will pertaining to these matters.** It is my belief that each person has a unique perspective of God's will and interpretations of His Word and Laws. Members of individual religious denominations will usually share the same viewpoints on a range of subjects. However, I'm not sure that any two people share the same vision of God.

In trying to acknowledge and recognize sin in today's environment, many will challenge that changes to the interpretations of God's law are not unprecedented in the Bible and Church history. This is particularly true when comparing the Mosaic Laws of the Old Testament to the 'New Testament Law' preached by Jesus. When the Pharisees were out to trap or trick Jesus, they would often test Him regarding Mosaic Law. Jesus often countered their attacks by rebuking the Jewish Pharisees and High Priests for their lack of understanding and obedience to the true meaning of the Scriptures and God's Law.

One example is when Jesus was asked why Moses allowed men to divorce (Deut 24:1-4). He responded: *"... Because of your hardness of heart, Moses permitted you to divorce your wives; but from the beginning, it was not this way. And I say to you whoever divorces his wife, except for immorality, and marries another woman commits adultery."–Matthew 19:8-9*

Jesus explains that during the time of Moses, men's hearts were hardened to the true meaning of God's message concerning marriage, divorce, and adultery, and permitted divorcing their wives. He then put us all on notice that these Old Testament practices of the past were allowed but no longer applicable and relayed God's true (more strict) intentions in one simple sentence (verse 9). The words of Jesus were unambiguous. Yet, in society today and even in most Christian churches, divorce and remarriage are widely accepted (more on 'divorce' in Part III). We should note that in the time of Jesus, women were not allowed by Jewish law to divorce their husbands. So how would His words apply today? It seems the actual intent behind His message is God expects marriages to be a lifetime commitment by both husband and wife. Let's consider this discrepancy between Mosaic Law and the teachings of Jesus. Some might claim this is evidence to support that certain aspects of God's Law, and consequently the definition of sin, have changed. Here in this situation, we see Jesus bringing stricter guidelines for God's people to follow.

We can also observe examples of Jesus contradicting some of the Pharisee's strict interpretations of Old Testament Law by taking a more lenient approach to Jewish 'man-made traditions.' These include Jesus and His disciples being accused by the Pharisees of working/taking too many steps on the Sabbath (Mark 2:23-28) and healing a blind man on the Sabbath (John 9:1-41). Despite their stature and position as Jewish Church leaders, here we see again in these instances the Pharisees were sometimes blind to the actual truth and intent of God's Laws. Looking at our Church and its leadership today, it is easy to see similarities in the 'traditions' employed over the centuries that have no proper basis in Scripture. Jesus gets his point across toward the end of John's story, describing the healing of the blind man. "Those of the Pharisees who were with Him heard these things and said to Him 'We are not blind too are we?' Jesus said to them 'If you were blind, you would have no sin; but since you say 'We see,' your sin remains" (John 9: 40-41)

The letter to the Hebrews in the New Testament confirms what God said in the book of Jeremiah the prophet about the days of the 'New Covenant.' 'After those days, says the Lord; I will put My laws upon their heart and on their mind I will write them' (Heb 10:16; ref Jer 31:33; Rom 2:12-16). Here God promises if we become familiar with the true teachings of the Scriptures, His laws will become written into our hearts and minds and we will come to a higher level of understanding. **Wisdom in the ways and will of the Father are the key aspects to discerning our sins as we perform our examinations of conscience.**

Probably one of the most famous confrontations Jesus encountered is when approached by the Pharisees about what is the most important commandment. It is here that Jesus provides us with two straightforward Laws to follow: "You shall Love the Lord your God with all your heart, and with all your soul, and with all your mind. This is the great and foremost commandment. The second is like it: you shall love your neighbor as yourself. On these two commandments depend the whole Law and the Prophets" (Matthew 22:37-40) Jesus puts into perspective that these two basic ideologies incorporate all of God's commandments. While many of us are very familiar with this passage, I think we often tend to 'gloss over' the first part of these simple truths that we must, above all, love God first.

Many Catholics I know share the belief that if we are 'good' to our family, friends, and neighbors around us, we will earn a spot in heaven. While that's certainly part of it, we tend to diminish the most important ('great and foremost') commandment Jesus gave us. There aren't many of us that have to look much past the first commandment given by God to Moses and restated by Jesus to identify the pride we have in our hearts and the false 'gods' we have before us every day. Money, career, sexual lust, sports, food, TV, computers, cell phones, alcohol, and drugs are just some of the worldly devices that are so present to us today, distracting us from spending time in loving devotion to God. Even our own family can sidetrack our devotion. Jesus describes this in Luke 14:26. Note that some biblical translations of this passage use the word 'hate' within the context of the verse. For example, in the King James translation: 'if anyone comes to me and hates not his father and mother, wife and children….' (KJV21). While other versions substitute the phrase 'does not love me more than' for 'hate not.' Matthew 19:29 and Mark 10:29 are related verses. Jesus was trying to get the point across that we must put Him before all else, and even our own family can distract us from becoming His loyal bond-servants and disciples.

The examples mentioned above lead some to contend that the Bible contains contradictions and is subject to different interpretations, depending on the era. So why can't we just make our own 'adjustments' and evaluations to God's Laws and dictate for ourselves what is sin and what isn't?

One of my favorite books of the Bible is the Letter of Paul to the Romans, which I've heard sometimes referred to as 'The Blueprint to Salvation.' Paul writes this letter to the newly formed church in Rome, prior to

IV WHAT IS SIN?

his first visit there. We believe during that period that the Roman Church comprised a mix of Jewish converts and Gentiles. Addressing the Jewish segment of this audience, he wrote the themes in the letter with frequent references to the 'Law' and Old Testament characters. As an example, he compares Jesus to both Adam and Abraham.

Paul does a great job expanding on the testimony of Jesus and His guidance concerning the Law. A major point hammered across several times in the first eight chapters of Romans (and many of his other letters as well) is that our salvation is not based on how well we adhere to and obey God's Old Testament Laws, but on our **saving faith and trust in Jesus Christ** and His death on the cross as payment for the penalties of our sins. It is this faith in Jesus's ultimate sacrifice and not any good works that we might do that declares us fully righteous and 'not guilty' before God for the sins we have committed against Him. Paul projects the philosophy that the Law exists mainly to show us we are all sinners, disobedient, and in need of God's mercy. 'As it is written, There is none righteous, not even one' (Rom 3:10). Here, Paul references excerpts of the Old Testament book of Psalms 14:1-3 and 53:1-4. Emphasis placed on the concept that 'good' people do not achieve their salvation by being good is repeated throughout Paul's letters. Stressed in his writings is we cannot judge our salvation based primarily on our good and bad deeds, but on the level of our faith and relationship with God, the Father. This, combined with our belief and trust in Jesus' sacrifice at Calvary as justification and payment for our sins, gives us the full benefit of Christ's righteousness in God's eyes and completes the package. Paul's teachings strongly reinforce the first commandment given to us by Jesus.

Brought up in the Catholic faith, I came to understand 'faith' and saying 'I believe' to be the same thing. Faith is so much more than that. Terms associated with real 'saving faith' include justification, sanctification, righteousness, obedience, spiritual hunger, and becoming a 'slave' to our Lord and Master, Jesus Christ. For more on this please see our series, '*Unwrap-*

ping God's Mystery of Salvation by Faith' on the blog page of our website: https://www.voicesoflaity.org/blog

As it was at first for me, I know this concept may be a bit of overload and difficult to grasp for many Roman Catholics, especially those that may have had a similar upbringing to mine in the faith and have not actively studied the Bible. It is one of God's great mysteries revealed to us through the Apostle Paul. The more we read and study the Scriptures, especially the New Testament, understanding and solving this mystery becomes clearer to us. These philosophies have become rooted as the cornerstone of my beliefs and are vital in coming to a better understanding of God's message and plan for me. My life is dedicated to a renewed focus on evangelization through reading, studying, and meditating on His Word. We cover in more detail 'salvation by faith' and its association to our works and deeds in Part III.

There's no doubt some will argue strongly against and question this philosophy of salvation by faith, holding steadfast in the belief so long as you are 'good' and follow Catholic traditions, your salvation is secured.

Others may interpret Paul's teachings by saying: 'OK, if the basis of our salvation is our love for God and faith in Jesus's death on the cross as payments for my sins, then I can choose purposely to disobey God's Laws at will or make up my own rules and still be saved.' In his wisdom, Paul expects these viewpoints to arise from members of the Roman Church and knocks them down immediately (Rom 6: 1-23). In chapters 6 and 7, Paul explains and reinforces that when we are spiritually baptized into faith in Christ, our old sinful-self dies with Him and it brings us to freedom from the slavery of sin. To forgo our earthly desires and freedoms and instead, through faith, become slaves to Our Lord and Master Jesus Christ, takes a monumental commitment. Once we've achieved a renewed relationship with God through the redemption of Christ, sin is dead to us and should be the farthest thing from our mind. If we truly love God with our whole hearts, minds, and souls as Jesus has instructed us to, then the road to holiness and following the commandments will be ingrained in us, and should be nothing short of second nature. Going to Mass or services on Sunday is a straightforward decision. We put our lustful thoughts and actions behind us. Mistreating, judging, preaching gossip and hate, or causing violence to family, friends, or any of those around us, becomes a foreign concept. Spending time with, listening to, giving glory and thanks to, and interacting with God now becomes the top focus and priority in our lives.

As we conclude this chapter, I'd like to reinforce this point with you one more time. To make a complete examination of conscience, we should search our souls not only for what we are doing wrong, but what are we doing right? What needs to change in our lives so that putting God first now becomes a priority? What have I done to help my neighbor or those less fortunate than me? If God were to ask me 'what have you done for *Me* lately,' how would I respond? What have I done to spread the Good News of salvation to others? How can I serve God?

During my soul searching, it was easy for me to identify that missing Mass was a sin against God, but one that was relatively simple to repent from and remedy. This was not a sin done consciously to shun God, but the result of my estranged relationship with Him. This was a sin easy for me to recognize. For many of us, there will be a genuine struggle in confronting the sins in our lives we need to repent from. How will we go about the process of repentance and reconciliation? Here are three suggestions I hope will help:

Use God's Word, the Bible, as your primary source of reference. Internet bible subject searches are very helpful (i.e. "Bible references to fornication...") in identifying God's point of view on the sins you have identified. Then seek God and His Holy Spirit to help guide you through repentance and reconciliation.

Consider your thoughts and actions and whether they give glory to you vs. glory to God.

Pray for continued guidance from the Holy Spirit.

I hope this chapter has you at least considering no matter where you are in life and your spiritual journey, that **each waking day provides you with a forbearance of God's mercy, blessings, kindness, and opportunity for redemption** (Rom 2:4).

V

DREAD THE LOSS OF HEAVEN, PAINS OF HELL

"Do not fear those who are able to kill the body but are unable to kill the soul; but rather fear Him who is able to destroy both body and soul in hell."
Matthew 10:28

I took the words forming the title of this chapter from the traditional version of the 'Act of Contrition.' For those that may not remember, this is the prayer one would recite at the end of your confession to the priest before doing your penance. It is this version of the prayer that I still remember from my youth.

Observing the present-day world condition, it's hard to argue against the reality that the Devil has us just where he wants us. So many in today's society have fallen victim to Lucifer's lies and attacks. They show little to no fear of God's pending judgment or the eternal consequences of our sins. Two of the biggest lies that the Devil tells us are that salvation can be 'earned' through following a 'religion,' and the measure of your success in life is based on your material gains and status and not on the level of your devotion to God.

Satan has us convinced that Hell and eternal torment are reserved only for the worst of us, like Hitler, Saddam Hussein, Charles Manson, or notorious dictators, terrorists, murderers, and rapists. Or even worse, persuading us Hell does not even exist and there are no consequences for our transgressions against God. Your eternal future in Heaven, the Devil will have you believe, is a foregone conclusion. If you were baptized and are a 'good,' peace-loving person, God will welcome you into Heaven when your time here on earth is over.

A soul found absent of the 'fear of God' and His judgment may be in danger of falling into a life of perpetual sin. If we don't consider the serious consequences of failing to identify and repent from our transgressions against God, an examination of conscience becomes a futile process

The Church's complicity in the lackadaisical mindset in our culture toward judgment and eternal destiny has become increasingly obvious. Sermons compelling us to repentance and evangelization have become obsolete in the Church today. Instead, we receive sermons designed and delivered to make us feel 'comfortable.' Produced to accommodate worldly views and lifestyles of our modern day congregations.

Even Pope Francis recently stated that everyone, regardless of the status of your faith, is in the communion of saints: *'let's think about those who have denied the faith, who are apostates, who are the persecutors of the Church, who have denied their baptism: Are these also at home? Yes, these too. The blasphemers, all of them. We are brothers. This is the Communion of Saints.'* (2/5/22)

Let's ask ourselves, how many Catholics and Christians still legitimately believe in the existence of Hell and eternal torment? God would never send us to Hell for eternity just because we don't attend Mass, or take His name in vain, deceive and/or hurt others, or are having sexual relations outside the bonds of marriage, would He? It is important to mention here that Scripture tells us **God judges us first on our faith and then on our actions** (Matt 12:36; 2 Cor 5:10). He does not 'send you to Hell,' but **it is the choices we make** while here on earth that compel Him to execute His justice and judgment on us.

V DREAD THE LOSS OF HEAVEN, PAINS OF HELL

For me, it comes back to the premise discussed in the previous chapter that God does not judge us based on transgressions against His Law. Scrutiny of the messages delivered by St. Paul in his letters reveals that none of us can perfectly follow the Law and are therefore all guilty of violating it. My interpretation of New Testament writings makes me suspect those who will be eternally damned and tormented are the ones who ignore God, fall into a life of disobedience and sin, and cannot embrace with faith Jesus's ultimate sacrifice on the cross. It is those who devote their time and efforts to the 'gods' of this world, putting their own pleasure and glory above God's, that will pay the ultimate price. In Romans, Paul asks: 'Are you a slave for Christ or of your own appetite? (Rom 16:7)'

As part of our Christmas morning sermon this year, the priest said that 'our God is not a God of punishment, but only a God of love.' Has he read the Scriptures? Truth be told, most of God's punishments on humanity have proven to be measures of His love, hoping they bring us to repentance so that none may perish (John 3:16; 2 Peter 3:9). But make no mistake, these are God's punishments. There are so many instances recorded in the Bible, particularly in the Old Testament, of God's chastisement on His people. A perfect example of this is how the angel Lucifer inherited his eternal fate (Isa 14:12-15; Luke 10:17-18; 2 Peter 2:4; Eze 28:12-15). Once one of the most beautiful of God's created angels, his downfall was founded on vanity when deciding he was equal to or even above God. Are we mere humans not guilty of this same conceit and deserving of the same eternal fate when we distance ourselves from God, putting Him somewhere on the 'back burner' of our lives? How often do we claim for ourselves the glory and thanksgiving that should be directed to God? These are the fruits borne from pride and arrogance. Adam and Eve, Cain, the great flood, Moses being prohibited from entering the Promised Land, and the Jews in the desert are some examples of God's punishment revealed in just the first few books of the Bible.

When I was teaching 8th grade CCD Confirmation classes back in the early 1990s, a student asked me: 'What do you think it's like to be in Hell?' I paused for a moment to think about how I might try to put that in perspective for a 13-year-old and replied: 'Imagine you were sent to an inescapable prison for life where the guards will not protect you and there are no bars or cells to keep the other prisoners from doing whatever they want to you. Imagine the guards are even more vicious to you than your fellow inmates. The worst thing, though, is that no matter how much pain and torture you endure, you cannot die.' My goal was to put a little fear into the hearts of those paying attention. I likened it to 'Scared Straight,' a TV documentary series back then that embedded 'at risk' teenagers into prison for a brief period to provide for them a view of what prison life was like, hoping it would scare them into turning their lives around.

There are two books on Hell and eternal torment I recommend reading. First is 'Dante's Inferno' (part of the 'Divine Comedy' trilogy.) It has some very interesting concepts concerning the plight of the eternally damned. It is from this book that the phrase deemed to be inscribed over the gates of Hell, 'Abandon All Hope, Ye Who Enter Here,' originates. I'm not suggesting the content of 'Dante's Inferno' should be taken as 'gospel truth,' but it gives us cause for wonder.

The other is *'Saints Who Saw Hell and Other Catholic Witnesses to the Fate of the Damned' by Paul Thigpen* (Thigpen, 2019). In this book, you will find some interesting parallels in the stories of the different visions of Hell and torment recorded and told by different saints and witnesses. There are some similarities to Dante's work. One of the key points mentioned by the witnesses in this book is that the most intense torment of the damned is knowing that their fate is **eternal,** with no end or relief to the suffering.

Philosophers and church scholars, both past and present, have a wide range of views on the existence of Hell. Bishop Barron is a modern-day Catholic clergy involved in a ministry called 'Word on Fire.' If you are interested, there are numerous videos on his 'YouTube' channel covering the

V DREAD THE LOSS OF HEAVEN, PAINS OF HELL

existence of Hell. Here, he provides some perspectives from modern-day scholars and old-world saints. Bishop Barron comes up with the conclusion I believe many people have adopted, stating that 'we must consider the possibility that Hell exists.'

After looking at the number of materials the Bishop offers on his website, there is no doubt in my mind that his ministry may have brought many Catholics to a better understanding of both the Bible and their faith. Respectfully, I disagree with the Bishop on many issues, especially this one. If you scroll down to the comments below his videos on the existence of Hell, you see that many of his followers are in disagreement with his philosophy as well. His viewpoint, one that I've often heard preached, contradicts the teachings of Jesus, who many times in his ministry refers to the existence of Hell, a place of eternal punishment for those that shun God. It would take a full chapter to discuss these references, so I'll provide you with the following Bible verses to research:

Matthew 7:13-14
Matthew 13:24-43
Revelation 20:15
Matthew 10:28
Luke 16:19-31
Matthew 25:31-46
Luke 13:23-28

Bishop Barron and others that profess to the teachings that perhaps all of us go to heaven and those Catholics that believe them are traveling down a dangerous road. In denying the existence of Satan and Hell, they also diminish the significance of Christ's redemptive suffering and death on the cross. If there is no Satan or Hell, then all of humanity's life paths would lead to Heaven and no need for anyone to be a Christian.

To summarize His gospel messages, Jesus clarifies that there will be an eternal judgment. He also preaches about a hierarchy in terms of both reward and punishment. He describes judgement, punishment, and torment as being 'more tolerable' for some than others (Matt 11:22-24). One of His most famous quotes is "So the last shall be first and the first last." (Matthew 20:16). In Matthew 7:13-14, Jesus further tells us: 'Enter through the narrow gate; for the gate is wide, and the way is broad that leads to destruction, and there are many who enter through it. For the gate is small, and the way is narrow that leads to life and there are few who find it.' These teachings of Jesus are in direct contrast to the discussed notion everyone goes to heaven. How much easier it is for us to disregard this warning, taking the wide and well-traveled path that everyone else follows. Jesus in his ministry often clarified that it is not a simple task to be one of His disciples. Even to the point made previously that we must love Him more than our own families and be willing to give up all for Him (Matthew 10:37).

Satan likes to paint us a picture of God as One who is all-loving, merciful, and forgiving, no matter what we do or how much we ignore Him. While love, compassion, and forgiveness are truly part of God's divine nature, the side of Him that the Devil does not want us to see is a God that is jealous, righteous, angered by sin, and faithful to serving justice. If our clergy portrays to us a God who does not punish sin, why would they then be surprised to see our churches empty? What would be the point of leading a faithful Catholic/Christian life?

Consider all the tribulations Moses endured in leading the Israelites out of Egypt. Despite all he did to serve Him, we can observe how angry God became at Moses for what seemed like a relatively minor act of disobedience. After telling him he need only 'speak to it,' Moses, in an act of defiance, hit the rock in the desert twice to bring forth water (Numbers 20: 8-12). As punishment, and probably more of an example to His people, Moses and Aaron were banned by God from entering the Promised Land for this act.

You hear many people raise the point of how and why God would send punishments and plagues into our world today if He is such a loving God. History shows us He often uses these methods as the best way for Him to get our attention when we have fallen into states of flagrant disobedience and separation from Him. A look at the Old Testament provides a chronicle of examples displaying God's judgment on believers and non-believers. It shows us how God used evil leaders of powerful nations to rise and destroy Israel after the Jewish people turned their backs on Him. The Jews were constantly in alternating eras of triumph and despair. They would rise as conquerors and other times fall, becoming captive slaves. Their fate usually depended on their level of obedience and trust in God. Despite warnings from God's Old Testament prophets, the Jews, in times of prosperity, would often overindulge in God's blessings. They became emboldened, no longer feeling the need to abide by his Laws, trust in Him for all that they had, or fear His judgment. Sound familiar? As Israel sinned against God, He unleashed judgment on His people by allowing the Egyptians, Assyrians, Babylonians, and eventually the Romans to enslave and rule over them. It is a never-ending cycle.

Another influential book I strongly suggest to you is *'The Paradigm' by Jonathan Cahn* (Cahn, 2017). The author provides an amazing paradigm or 'comparison model.' He details the similarities between the kings and queens in power during God's judgment on Israel and Judah after the reign of King Solomon, to the political leaders in the United States here in the 21st century.

Much like the founding of our great nation was based on godly principles, God built the great nation of Israel and His Holy Temple during the reigns of King David and King Solomon. But after the death of King Solomon, the Jewish people ended up in the divided kingdoms of Judah and Israel. Eventually, both kingdoms turned their hearts away from God, engaging in all kinds of sin under the leadership of ungodly kings and queens. They became complacent in their riches, directing their worship and building temples to the worldly idols of Queen Jezebel and the god Baal. Despite pleadings and warnings from many prophets (Isaiah, Ezekiel, Jeremiah, etc.), the Jews refused to repent from their evil ways. God eventually imposed his judgment by allowing King Nebuchadnezzar of Babylon to utterly destroy both Israel and Judah, and even God's own Holy Temple and the City of Jerusalem. The people of the Jewish nation subsequently lost all their riches and were committed to slavery. Did God allow this because He did not love His Chosen People? No, it was just the opposite. He loved the Jewish nation as His people, but had to get their attention so they would come back to Him.

Part of the idolatry of the gods Molech and Baal embraced by the Jews during this period included the burning sacrifice of innocent young male children to this god. The murder and death of these infant children were not punishable by civil law. A related paradigm in our society is the practice of abortion, now so commonplace in our western civilization. Jeremiah, under God's direction, proclaimed this message to the people of Judah: 'Your clothing is stained with the blood of the innocent and the poor. Brazenly, you murder without a cause. And yet you say,' "I haven't done a thing to anger God. I'm sure He isn't angry!" 'I will punish you severely because you say, "I haven't sinned!"' (Jeremiah 2:34-35) (Life Application Bible, 1988). If you have the time I encourage you to read the many other references (listed below) in the book of Jeremiah that sound very much like the mindsets of today's society regarding the complacent attitudes and proclamations of innocence the Jewish people had toward their sins against God (Jeremiah 3:3-5; 5:8-10; 6:14-15; 7:8; 8:6-13).

While the Psalms tell us that the Lord is kind, merciful, and slow to anger (Psalms 103 8:18; 145:8), we see the example above of a time when God could no longer be patient and forced to exercise anger and judgment on His people to get their attention and lead them away from their sinful habits. That God would even ordain the destruction of His own Holy City of Jerusalem and the Holy Temple should give us concern about what may be in store for us. Through my prayers, I believe we are not too far off from this same fate as a nation unless we as a people and a Church heed the call to repentance, turn from our assertions of innocence, and admit that we have sinned grievously against God. While I pray for these things to happen, I'm not very optimistic and feel trends will continue to move in quite the opposite direction, in particular with the younger generations of our society.

Like the Jewish nation experienced over 2500 years ago, there will be warnings from God that most of us will ignore. Could it be that 9/11 was one of God's first warnings? Writing today in 2021, the world is gripped in a mass hysteria over the Corona Virus and financial markets are collapsing. Worldwide travel has come to a grinding halt. 'Social distancing' is the new buzzword now guided by world leaders to isolate ourselves from others to prevent the spread of this disease until this phenomenon passes. What would our world be like if we feared God's judgment as much as we fear this virus?

Probably the most important lesson I've learned on judgment is that it is certainly not our job to judge others. Jesus made this quite clear in one of his more notable quotes: 'judge not, lest ye be judged' (Matthew 7: 1-3). Often we hear questions like 'Do all Jews go to Hell because they don't accept Jesus as their savior?' Those who follow Islam or Buddhism? From my point of view, it is a waste of energy to concern ourselves with debating questions like these. God will judge all of us as He sees fit. By providing us a perfect path to salvation through our redemption in His Son Jesus Christ, our focus should be on making as many people as we can know His path and plan. Religious affiliation, or where an individual is in their relationship with God, should not restrict or dictate our testimony.

Is there any religious denomination in the world that 'perfectly' knows the mind of God? Interprets His Word without error? How would we know that was the case? Is it the Catholic faith that has it all right, the Baptists, the Lutherans? While agreeing on some basic beliefs, we can argue for eternity over the differences of philosophies between Christian sects and denominations. These debates have been going on since the very founding of the Church. To what end will that bring us?

Judging other individuals is probably one of humanity's biggest flaws. Many will tout individual Bible verses to condemn someone. They try to prove their case on a certain topic and close their minds to any who would contradict or oppose them. During His ministry, Jesus did not 'hang out' with the leaders of the Jewish church and community. He acquainted himself with sinners, bringing them the message of salvation (Mark 2: 15-17). He healed many sinners both physically and spiritually and often would instruct them to 'go and sin no more' (John 8:11).

One quote that has always stuck in my mind regarding judging other people is when Jesus speaks in Matthew 7:4-5 "How can you say to your brother, 'Let me take the speck out of your eye', and behold, the log is in your own eye?"

I came across a great example related to this passage recently that I'd like to share. An old friend of mine, a member of the LGBTQ community, constantly spews messages of hate on Facebook and Twitter directed toward President Trump, Republicans, the Christian right, and anyone who agrees with and/or supports their policies. This probably doesn't surprise you. Yet as he preaches this hatred, he will, rightfully so, condemn vigorously any hateful comments made against the LGBTQ population. It just feels so hypocritical to both preach and condemn hatred, but it is something we see so much of in our society today. If we look at Luke 6:32-36 and Matt 5:46 Jesus tells us it is easy to love those that love us or agree with us, even sinners do that, but our true reward comes from loving those that we disagree with, insult us, and especially those whom we feel are living outside of God's will.

In concluding the discussion on eternal fate and judgement, here are the key points I think we need to pray for:

All of us will be judged when we die, and our eternal destiny will be determined by the degree of our devotion to God, and our faith in the saving redemption of His Son, Jesus Christ. In his first letter to the Corinthians, **St. Paul tells us God will save those who build their spiritual foundation on faith in Christ.** Then they will have their level of

V DREAD THE LOSS OF HEAVEN, PAINS OF HELL

eternal reward determined by putting their earthly works and deeds, used as the building blocks of their 'spiritual household,' through 'the fire' of God's judgement. (1 Cor 3:10-15).

Satan will continue to persuade us that there is no punishment for putting ourselves above God (like he did) and assures us we are all destined for Heaven. Once convinced, the Devil has done his job.

In His ministry, Jesus tells us many times that the road to Heaven is difficult. It directly contradicts the popular belief that almost everyone will inherit eternal reward. There needs to be a great sense of urgency to influence our family, friends, and all those around us. We must persuade them to repentance and rededication of their lives. Encourage them to becoming truly devoted to discerning, knowing, and carrying out the will of God.

It is not our job to judge others, but to let God be the only judge. The primary thing for us to focus on is preaching to everyone Christ crucified for our sins (1 Corinthians 2:2; Galatians 6:14).

We need to show love and respect to all of those around us, even more so to those that we may feel are enemies against us, or have conflicting points of view. True Catholics/Christians have no room for hate in their hearts.

The Jewish nations over 2500 years ago endured God's wrath and judgment because they failed to listen to God through the words of His prophets, pleading for them to repent. The next chapter will consider how we can listen to God and perhaps, as both individuals and a nation avoid the same fate.

VI
LISTENING TO GOD

"Blessed is the man who listens to me, watching daily at my gates, waiting at my doorposts. For he who finds me finds life and obtains favor from the Lord. But he who sins against me injures himself; all those who hate me love death."
Proverbs 8:34-36

In opening this most important chapter, I feel it vital to stress the need to take a step away from the spiritual 'tunnel vision' ingrained in us from our Catholic upbringing. Let us consider keeping an open heart and mind to listening to and engaging in spiritual perspectives from outside our Catholic Church. It is my solemn belief I never would have achieved the level of spirituality and closeness to God that I enjoy today had I not embraced these external teachings and viewpoints.

Without question, the most influential person in my life's spiritual journey has been Dr. Charles Stanley. He is the former pastor of the First Baptist Church of Atlanta, Georgia, and spiritual director of 'In Touch Ministries ™.' There was an era of my life that I self-describe as my 'spiritual awakening and renewal.' This was during the mid to late 1980s and early 1990s, while I was in my 30s and early 40s.

Dr. Stanley played an instrumental role in leading me to salvation through faith in Jesus Christ, and to a deeper and more intimate relationship with God. His weekly 'In Touch ™' broadcasts were 'must-see' television for both me and my wife every Sunday night. His teachings included a wide range of interesting biblical topics. I strongly encourage everyone to watch and listen to some of his teachings on 'YouTube™' or visit the In Touch™ website (www.intouch.org) to browse through the resources. Dr. Stanley, even now at age 86, continues today to preach influential gospel messages in his weekly broadcasts.

In my experience, one of the most powerful and impactful series presented by Dr. Stanley was entitled 'How to Listen to God' and is now available in book form (Stanley, How To Listen To God, 1985). In my heart, I feel this is such an important lesson to absorb for anyone trying to establish a deeper personal relationship and devotion to God. While Dr. Stanley presents this material more eloquently than I ever could, much of the remaining content in this chapter is based on his teachings.

As we go through our daily 'walk of life,' do we know or even care about what God's plan is for our life? Are we attentive to what God expects from us? Do we know the direction He is trying to point us in? It is so common for us in today's society to live our lives according to our own plans and give little thought to what God intends for us. After all, we don't enjoy giving up control because we surely know what's best for us. Perhaps we'll give an occasional look to God in prayer, but how will we ever know what God's plan is for us if we don't take the time to ask Him, and then listen attentively for His response (Psalms 32:8)? Many would agree that listening is the most critical attribute to the processes of communicating, learning, and understanding. As an example, Jesus often began his parables by getting the attention of the crowds to listen (Mark 4:1; 4:23; 7:14)

Most of us have probably come across that person who is always talking and never listens. They talk over others in conversations and while others are speaking, instead of listening, will plan in their heads what to say next. This person often can seem arrogant and annoying. Yes, I have to admit at times I am guilty of this myself. If we stop and think about it, many Christians can form these same habits of prayer. In our prayers, we may give thanks to God, ask Him for a particular blessing or two, pray for a loved one that is ill, or maybe even complain about a life situation that is not going too well for us. What we need to ask ourselves honestly is how much do we listen to God in our prayers? Is it a one-way or two-way conversation?

The concept of 'listening to God' can be challenging for a lot of us. Many have common questions about how God speaks to us. Will I hear an audible voice? Is it all just in my mind? Is it during our Sunday sermons? How do I know it is God and not Satan speaking to my heart? It is my goal in this chapter, based on lessons learned from Dr. Stanley and others, to help answer these questions, simplify the discerning process, and encourage you to develop and maintain a listening spirit.

We should note it right off the bat that God will not necessarily always tell us what we want to hear. Many times, He will tell us the exact opposite of what we want or expect to hear, making it so much more difficult to follow where He leads us on our life's path. There is a popular responsorial psalm we hear at Mass taken from Hebrews 3:15, referencing Psalms 95:7: "Today, if you hear His voice, do not harden your hearts, (as when they provoked me)." Why would we harden our hearts if we hear God speak to us? Precisely because He is not telling us what we want to hear, leading to rebellion against Him.

An obvious question you may have is: 'What are the best ways to listen to God and in what manner does He speak to His children today?'

The most evident and primary vessel of God's voice to us is His written Word, the Bible. I would challenge anyone to open their Bible to the Books of Proverbs, Psalms, Letters of St. Paul, etc. and just listen to God talking to your heart. No matter what book or section of the Bible you open to, just begin reading and you can't help but hear the Holy Spirit speaking to your soul. A suggestion I have for you is when you're finished reading and meditating on His Word, leave the Bible open in a conspicuous location in your home to the page that you read last. During your daily routine, each time you pass by the open Bible, imagine God speaking out to you from its pages saying: 'Hey, come here. I want to talk to you for a minute.'

Are you dealing with a specific issue where you are seeking God's help? In today's world, simple internet searches can bring you to related Bible verses in just a few brief minutes. There is a link for a site that I have found helpful at the end of this chapter, and there are many more like it. Are you feeling an overwhelming sense of anxiety? Just search for 'Bible references to anxiety.' Maybe you are experiencing fear or are involved in sexual immorality. Do you have problems with gluttony? Just about any issue that you are dealing with has related Bible verses that speak to it.

Another great tool in developing your listening skills is maintaining a prayer journal, jotting down both what you say to/ask of God, and what you believe He is saying to/asking of you. How has He answered your prayers from the past? The content of this book you are reading is a perfect example of putting the voice you hear from the Holy Spirit into writing. Record everyday events where you feel the hand of God working as He speaks to your prayers. We will see later on in this chapter how the circumstances in our daily lives reflect on how God speaks to us and how important it is for us to recognize them.

The second source that moves us toward listening to God is the Holy Spirit that dwells within us. Dr. Stanley describes the Holy Spirit as our 'radar' that detects, filters, and discerns the content of the voices we are hearing. It is so vital to realize how heavily we must rely on the Holy Spirit's guidance in helping us follow only those voices that are consistent with God's Law, Word, and will. If you are reading from the Bible, you can be pretty sure that what you are hearing is God speaking the truth to your heart.

Continuing, let's ask ourselves, who do we listen to most often? What type of medium has our greatest attention and impact on our lives? For

VI LISTENING TO GOD

most of us, it is our interactions with the world through TV, the internet, social media, cell phones, peers, etc. having the heaviest influence on our decisions, thoughts, and actions. Unless we change our focus away from listening to these worldly influences, we have little chance of hearing God speak to us over the noise. If we truly seek God's blessings and are dedicated to progressing toward a deeper relationship with Him, we must welcome the Holy Spirit into our hearts and focus our listening on Him. I can't tell you how many times in my own life that the Holy Spirit clarified that the voice I'm hearing is not from God, but yet I still followed it in disobedience. You'll find it is so much easier to make excuses and follow **your** crafted life plan rather than take the tougher road spending time to discern the truth from the Holy Spirit and follow God's chosen plan for you.

So, as we experience the conditions of everyday life, when not having our nose in the Bible, how do we determine if what we are hearing is from God or not? There are two basic tests we can apply when trying to recognize, evaluate, and act on a situation. Ask the Holy Spirit within you: Is the decision and/or action I am about to make consistent with the Word of God? Is this path something that gives glory to God or myself? Is what I am about to do worthy of God's blessings? One of the first lessons that I would always teach my confirmation CCD classes was that 'selfishness is the opposite of holiness.' That said, it can sometimes be hard to 'practice what you preach.'

We'll look at one more source that God uses to speak to us, and that is through our life circumstances. There are two sides to this coin. First, if we are following in God's path and listening carefully to Him, we can recognize and acknowledge the blessings and rewards we receive as God speaks to us.

A great example of this in my own life is when I began to give a weekly tithe of time, treasure, and talent to the Church and various charities. Before developing this habit, like many Catholics, when the time came for the Offering at Mass, I would drop maybe a dollar or two in the collection basket. This was my 'sacrifice' and I never gave it a second thought. It was what most everyone else did. The more I studied God's Word, the more I realized

I was 'slighting' Him. This is what I gave as thanks for all His blessings? No wonder my family's finances were at rock bottom. It was no simple task cultivating a new custom of tithing (more on tithing later in the book), given the poor condition of our finances back then. Note that our financial situation did not turn around instantly. Instead, slowly and steadily, things improved, going from near bankruptcy to a point where I secured a steady job, could help my three children get through college, and even start saving for retirement. In my heart, I felt God speaking to me through all these wonderful blessings. If I hadn't been 'listening,' how easy it would have been to miss these great blessings from God. In addition, it would have been simple for me to be prideful, taking all the credit for this turnaround myself. The point to stress here is to be on constant alert and persistent with ears, minds, and hearts opened to God's voice.

Then, of course, there is the other side of the coin. If we are not attentive to God's voice and straying from the path that He intends for us, He will frequently try to get our attention by speaking to us through our circumstances. Often these events will not be 'pretty,' and in fact, can be painful. If we are true believers, we should strive to recognize God's voice not only in blessings but in hardships and adversity. More often than not, instead of recognizing these difficulties as coming from God to get our attention, we may look at these situations as just 'bad luck,' or an unfortunate 'twist of fate.' We may even blame or curse God for what He has done to our circumstances. How often in the Old Testament do we see the Jewish nation refusing to listen to God and then enduring the horrible fates of destruction and slavery for many generations?

Remember that God has control of our lives and can deliver His message to us today in many ways. It can be through other people, even those who may not be friends or acquaintances. As the Jewish nation learned, it certainly can be through our enemies. It could be by an everyday course of event, or the internet and social media. There is no limit to the number of avenues God might take to reach us. We just have to be actively listening for it.

To adopt and develop a listening spirit, there needs to be an urgency to make it a priority in our lives to do so. Our daily life practice should be one that hungers for a constant conversation with God. When something out of the ordinary, big or small, in our daily routine occurs, we should ask: 'What is God trying to tell me here?' Or 'What does the Bible say about this decision I'm making?' Whenever experiencing any overwhelming negative emotions like anxiety, fear, depression, etc., go to God's written Word and see what He has to say about it.

One thing you will notice when you cultivate these listening habits is that God's Holy Spirit will start 'talking your ear off.' Some nights I lie in bed trying to get to sleep and the Holy Spirit will continuously stimulate me with so many inspirations. Then I try, as best I can, to translate these insights into my writing. Being in an ongoing conversation with the one true living God is such a powerful experience to be enjoyed.

It is my prayer that you will come to know the Spirit and let Him provide you with the guidance and encouragement that comes with listening to God resulting in the living of a Godly life, being an example to others in sharing the gospel, and receiving God's grace.

In concluding this chapter, I will leave you with a few scripture readings related to this subject.

Proverbs 4: - Notice how many times the word 'listen' is mentioned in this chapter.

Psalm 25: 4-10 – Here David speaks of staying on God's path.

Proverbs 8: 32-36 – Persistence in listening to God.

As we move forward to the next chapter, we will look at the principal way in which God speaks to us through his Holy Word, the Bible.

http://www.openbible.info/topics/

VII

THE BIBLE

"For I am not ashamed of the Gospel, for it is the power of God for salvation to everyone who believes.... For in it, the righteousness of God is revealed from faith to faith; as it is written, 'But the righteous man shall live by faith.'"
Romans 1:16-17

Referring again to my teaching days of 8th-grade confirmation classes, I made it my mission every year to teach this age group as much about the Bible as I could. After a comprehensive review of the books of the Bible at the beginning of the year, as time went on occasionally I would divide the class into teams and run classroom scavenger hunts where they would have to know how to look up Bible verses to get letters/words as clues to find hidden treasures. It was an effective tool in at least familiarizing these early teens with God's Word. As part of the process to impress upon them the importance of the Bible, I would always repeat a story I'd heard from one of the TV evangelists that went like this: 'Imagine when you fall asleep tonight an angel appears to you in your dreams and hands you a gold-laced envelope. The angel tells you that inside are instructions to follow that will make you happy, wealthy, and wise for all eternity. The following morning, as you awaken, you see the same gold envelope that appeared in your dream sitting there on top of your dresser. Would you ignore the letter and just leave it there going about your normal daily routine, or would you read it? That golden envelope would contain a letter with three simple words 'Read the Bible.'

Growing up attending Catholic school and beyond, reading the Bible was neither encouraged nor discouraged by the Church. You got to hear most of your scripture readings at Sunday Mass. Sometimes the priest would base his sermon on these readings and sometimes not. The nuns taught us the 'major' Bible stories 'Noah's ark,' 'Adam and Eve,' 'Sermon on the Mount,' 'the Resurrection,' etc. but rarely read the stories directly from the Bible.

Later in life, I came to realize that I'd missed so much of the in-depth truths and philosophies revealed in the gospels, St. Paul's letters, the Old Testament, and other scripture writings. As it was for the faithful in previous centuries, we were led to believe that the Church had the one correct interpretation of the scriptures. There was no pressing need to read the entire Bible. You need only follow the catechism, engage in the sacraments, the Church 'traditions,' and surely you would be on the right pathway to salvation. Praise God that through enlightenment from ministers outside of the Church, I became so much better acquainted with His Word. Through no fault of their own, I believe so many Catholics have been deprived of many wonderful blessings they could have gained by studying and meditating on the fullness of God's Word.

If you have never read the Bible in its entirety, I eagerly encourage you to do so. From my point of view, what better way to discern the will and mind of God? To **understand** His ultimate plan for us as individuals and humankind. The Word of God establishes the benchmark by which we should measure the legitimacy of the philosophies and ideologies that are constantly being preached to us and practiced by the 'world' today.

Even the spiritual truths and policies professed by the Catholic Church should be evaluated and scrutinized based on the standards found in God's Word. If you are not familiar with the Word of God in its totality, how can you make a confident judgment regarding what is acceptable vs. non-acceptable behavior in the mind of God?

If you don't own a modern version of the Bible, let me suggest you acquire either a 'Life Application' or 'Study Bible.' I have found that these styles of Bibles add great value to helping understand the Word of God as it applies to our current life circumstances. For over 35 years, my wife and I have used the same Life Application Bible. Its pages are filled with underlines, notes and the leather binding is tearing. Deciding it was finally time for a new Bible, we just recently purchased *'The MacArthur Study Bible'* (MacArthur, 2020). I was so excited to read it and jumped right into my favorite book, the Letter of Paul to the Romans. Without going into great detail here, I can tell you this study Bible is simply amazing.

Typically, Life Application and Study Bibles have cross-referenced bible verses in their margins. These citations point to additional locations in the Bible with related topics, and/or if the Bible author is relating to a particular scripture verse. You may also find notes associated with specific verses at the bottom of the pages. Examples of what you may find there are explanations for Greek/Hebrew translations or putting content into a modern-day context. It is my recommendation that you treat these comments and explanations as 'tools' for digging deeper into the meaning of the verses. Consider them 'food for thought' rather than adopting them as 'gospel truth.' Recently, I learned there is a King James Version (KGV) of the Life Application Bible but have not had a chance yet to review it.

While it is certainly up to you, the order you choose to read the Holy Scriptures, I recommend the following sequence:

Gospel of Luke
Gospel of John
Acts of the Apostles
Letters of St. Paul–Starts with Romans
All other Epistles
Remaining 2 Gospels of Mark and Matthew

Old Testament
Revelations

I suggest this sequence because I believe we should first read, observe, and come to understand the life and Words of Jesus. Reading one of the 'synoptic' gospels (Luke) and then John's gospel will give you a diversion of perspectives from among the four gospels. The Acts of the Apostles (written mostly by Luke) gives you a historical perspective of the Early Church. The rest of the sequence should fit nicely for you.

An interesting note to know is that Luke, who was not an apostle, was identified by Paul to be a physician (Col 4:14) and we can assume he had a background in science. His written Gospel and Acts reflect a more historical, fact-based perspective than John's theme of portraying Jesus's deity. Luke, compared to the authors of the other synoptic Gospels, pays particular attention to the healing ministry of Jesus, as you might expect from a physician. John wrote his Gospel mostly for the Greeks, known for worshiping many gods. He wanted to push across to his audience that Jesus was, with the Father and the Holy Spirit, the eternal one and only true God.

Before reading a particular book in the Bible, there is a significant benefit to familiarizing yourself with its background. Who is the author of the book? To whom was it written, the audience? When was it written? What are the major themes and lessons the author is trying to portray in the verses? The answers to these questions give you a much better understanding of the book's content as you read it. The Life Application and Study Bibles in most cases contain this information as summaries at the beginning of each book. Some books may even have a short story that relates to the topic (s) discussed by the author.

Did you know the four gospels were written for four different audiences? Each had a specific message to help their intended readers grasp the person of Jesus Christ and His preaching. You may have heard that St. Paul wrote some of his letters from a prison cell. The details of all the books in

VII THE BIBLE

the Bible would require a new manuscript. If interested, you can always do an internet search on any individual book of the Bible for specifics related to the content.

Many Protestant denominations proclaim the Bible is the exclusive (sola scriptura) and ultimate final say relating to the Word of God. Nothing added or taken away. They sometimes base this claim on the verse at the end of John's Revelation "I testify to everyone who hears the words of the prophecy of this book: if anyone adds to them, God will add to him the plagues which are written in this book; and if anyone takes away from the words of the book of this prophecy, God will take away his part from the Tree of Life and from the Holy City, which are written in this book" (Rev 22:18-19). Looking carefully at this passage, we see this was an angel speaking to John about the writing of his Book of Revelation and not the entire Bible, as obviously the Bible was not compiled yet.

There are many versions of the Bible. Some of the Old Testament books included in the Catholic versions of the Bible are excluded from the Protestant version. Who knows what the authentic version is? There are many books and scriptural texts that were 'voted out' and purposely excluded for various reasons when members of the early Church compiled what they believed were the 'sacred scriptures.' They often cited questions of authenticity. The Book of Enoch from the Old Testament days, the Gospel of Thomas, and the Apocalypse (vision) of Paul are just a few of the examples of writings that were spiritual in nature and may have been candidates for inclusion into the Bible. More recently (the 1940s and 1950s), the Dead Sea Scrolls were discovered in the Qumran Caves in the Judean desert near the Dead Sea. The content of the scrolls added much to the validity of the writings of the Old Testament. I guess the point I'd like to get across here is that while the Bible remains our main source of God's Word, we should understand there may be some value in reading other scriptural (apocrypha) books and texts to enhance and supplement the teachings we receive from the Bible in coming to know God.

To this day, there is much debate amongst biblical scholars as to the exact origins of the Bible as it appears in its current form(s). Even though there is no direct formal evidence of this, some believe that most of the Bible, as it appears in its current state, was in place before the Council of Nicea in 325 A.D. Support for this theory comes from the fact that the Roman Emperor Constantine (the Great) called together Christian leaders from around the known world to this Council, famous for the Nicene Creed. Emperor Constantine commissioned 50 copies of the Holy Scriptures to be scribed and distributed so that there would be a sole source of scripture for Christians to follow. Other scholars will say that the Bible was not completed until the Council of Rome (382 A.D.), or the Council of Hippo (393 A.D.). Others say as late as the Council of Trent in the mid-1500s where the Vulgate, a Latin translation of the Bible from the 4th century (St. Jerome), was deemed to be the official Bible of the Catholic Church.

Then some will dispute the authenticity and accuracy of the Bible entirely. There are some arguments that are worth considering. Would you be able to defend these points with your own counterpoints?

If someone says that the 'Lord spoke to them' do we automatically believe it to be true? (i.e. Moses, Samuel, Prophets, St. Paul) Could these be just dreams?

Christians proclaim the Bible as 'the Word of God,' while Muslims say the same for the Koran. Does saying something is 'the Word of God' make it so?

There is a consensus the Gospels of Matthew and Mark were written around 50-70 A.D. Completed before the destruction of the temple by the Romans in 70 A.D. Why did it take over 15 years from the time of His death to put the life of Jesus down into writing? Wouldn't written details on the life of Jesus have been beneficial to conversions in the ancient Christian churches?

A large segment of biblical scholars believe the actual gospel authors were anonymous and eventually 'assigned' to names of Jesus' disciples many years

VII THE BIBLE

after they were written. Many also claim much of the content of New Testament writings was edited. Purposely synchronized, and/or embellished by church members other than the indicated authors to provide effect and consistency. Except for a few small samples, none of the original New Testament manuscripts exist. This means that all of what we now read in the New Testament was probably copied (and/or recopied) by someone other than the original designated authors. It certainly leaves the door open to the possibilities of personal influence and editing.

Another argument regarding the validity of Jesus as the Messiah is that while performing all these great miracles, healings, feeding thousands, raising people from the dead, etc. why is there so little historical evidence of Jesus outside of the New Testament writings?

How can we be so sure the Resurrection actually happened and not fabricated by the Apostles to 'save face' after the horrible death of Jesus on the cross?

Was St. Paul's experience on the road to Tarsus a hallucination and then his subsequent blindness, (Acts 9:3-9) the results of an epileptic seizure? Was epilepsy the sickness or 'thorn in his side' that he often spoke of? (2 Cor 12:7-10) Is this why Luke (physician) accompanied Paul on some of his journeys?

As you might imagine, besides the items mentioned above, there are many theories and challenges out there from atheists and agnostics about the validity of the Christian Bible.

To be clear, there is no doubt in my mind that the Bible is the inspired written Word of God. Regardless of how the final version of the Bible came to be, I believe God always had His hand involved with the process of its compilation. Is there a mandate, because it's the Word of God that it has to be perfect with no errors, inconsistencies, or contradictions? For me, it has come down to being open-minded. Written by humans often working off handed down oral traditions that were sometimes hundreds of years old (Genesis) rather than eye witness or real-time accounts is something to be looked at. We should also consider that there is a good deal of symbolism used in Genesis, Revelations, and some of the prophetic books that are certainly left open to interpretations. Just as no two people will share the same vision of God, so too I believe no two people will interpret the entire Bible exactly the same. I'll end this chapter with some of my perspectives on the Bible and how I think we should examine it in today's world.

While studying and understanding the details of the Bible gives us great insight into the mind of God, I believe it is also important for us to take a step back and contemplate a more general view of God's message to us. As previously discussed, Jesus often rebuked the Pharisees and Jewish leaders for overthinking things and not understanding God's scriptures, messages, and laws. They would get so bogged down in the details of their interpretations of the Law (i.e. # of steps you could take on the Sabbath, animal sacrifices, etc.) that they missed the bigger picture. We can see the Catholic Church is just as guilty on many fronts. We often hear biblical scholars make statements like 'the Greek translation of this Bible phrase is…,' or 'the Hebrew translation is…,' or 'in Revelations this symbolizes….' Although not trying to undermine the importance of acknowledging details, I feel strongly that Jesus wanted us to simplify our understanding of God's Word and Laws. The big picture is **God is love** and we need to come to know, love, and **put Him first in our lives** (Matt 6:33). We must honor and listen to Him obeying the Laws and commands He has written in our hearts. Then second, we must pay forward and extend our love for God to our neighbors by bringing His message to them. While these principles may seem simple, they are extremely difficult to adhere to and follow.

Satan and society are consistently 'talking and shouting over' the Word of God, leading us to crave and worship the things of this world, putting ourselves above both God and our neighbors. For all those living in selfishness, ignorance and unrepentant disobedience to God, Jesus warns there will be judgment and eternal torment. The exception being those very few

VII THE BIBLE

that exercise sincere repentance and come to eternal life through the 'narrow gate.' (Matt 7:13-14).

Proceeding to take an overview of the Bible, let's first examine the Old Testament. Here we discover a detailed account of Creation, followed by the stories of the Jewish nation falling in and out of God's favor. It reveals their experiences in both victory and defeat. God's chosen people were subjected to His blessings and punishments. They usually corresponded to their level of commitment and devotion to Him and the Mosaic Laws He gave them. The Israelites, much like our culture today, drifted into sin and ignored God, especially when things were going well and His blessings were upon them. As they, over some time, would turn further and further away from Him, they were continually being beckoned to return to the Lord and embrace a spirit of repentance. These callings notably observed in the writings of the prophets (Isaiah, Jeremiah, Ezekiel, etc.) seek repentance from the people of Judah and Israel.

We can also categorize the Old Testament as a compilation of Jewish history, with several books containing historical accounts of the Jewish leaders and Kings (Samuel I & II, Kings I & II, Chronicles I & II). Books of praise (Psalms), wisdom (Proverbs), and prophecy (Daniel, Isaiah, etc.), complete the story of God's plan for identifying man's sin and preparing the world for the arrival of Our Savior, His Son, Jesus Christ.

As you browse through the Old Testament, you will recognize many of the great Bible stories that almost all of us remember from our youth. The accounts of Adam and Eve, Noah's Ark, Abraham and Isaac, David and Goliath, Daniel in the Lion's Den, King David, and many more contained there. You really can experience a higher level of appreciation for these stories as you examine more closely how the Hand of God was involved in these events.

As mentioned earlier, there is a high level of uncertainty concerning the actual written origins of the New Testament. This leads us to believe that the Apostles, in the early years of Christianity, proclaimed the events of Jesus's life and His preaching mostly through oral expression. Given the low literacy rates in those times, they probably did not feel an urgent need to put it all into writing immediately.

Proclamations of the life, teachings, miracles, death, and resurrection of Jesus were most likely 'slowly but surely' put into written words by various followers of Jesus and the Apostles. We know Luke accompanied St. Paul on some of his missions and Mark considered a disciple of St. Peter. From the writings of Luke (Gospel, Acts), it appears he spent a good deal of time gathering historical facts from the Apostles, disciples, and Mary, Mother of Jesus.

Further evidence that limited written accounts of the gospels existed in the early Church was St. Paul in his letters does not speak much about specifics in the 'life' of Christ. There is no comment on the parables and teaching quotes we see in the gospels. Instead, he dedicates his writings to emphasize the relevance of Christ crucified for our sins, the Resurrection, and salvation through faith.

There are several factors, I believe, contributing to the lack of historical evidence outside of the New Testament concerning the life of Jesus. We should keep in mind that the Jews were anxiously waiting for an earthly leader, a powerful Messiah resembling King David. Most believed if the savior were to come at that time in history, surely He would free them and Jerusalem from the bondage of Rome.

From the Jew's perspective, Jesus was not the first radical preacher to claim the title of the Messiah. Others came both before and after Jesus. Many of Jesus's detractors, past and present, claim He was Satanic, a magician, master hypnotist, anything but a real miracle worker and the 'Son of God.' Consider also that Jesus's followers made up just a small percentage of the total population of Israel. He may not have been quite as 'famous' as some parts of the gospels portray Him to be. It is probable that the vast majority of those who followed Him were not the most elite of Israel and were closer to being counted among the country's poor. His tragic death on the

VII THE BIBLE

cross served as the final blow to any hopes the Jews may have had that perhaps He was their 'deliverer.' These dynamics paved the way for the general assessment of His brief life from those living in those times to be one of just another false prophet laying claim to the title of Messiah. A life not worth mentioning again. Thinking about it, it took quite a while for those closest to Him, the Apostles, to put down into writing the events of His life.

Having bet everything on Jesus and lost, the disciples quickly went into hiding after the crucifixion for fear they would endure the same fate as Jesus if hunted down by the Romans. For two days and nights, we can only imagine the loss of hope and level of despair experienced by His closest followers. Then something happened... the greatest event in human history, the Resurrection! Jesus had risen from the dead. Reading all four gospel accounts of the Resurrection, they seem to be fairly consistent with all of them mentioning angels at the site of the empty tomb greeting the women that went to prepare the body with spices. However, it seems to be kind of strange that given the magnitude of this event, the descriptions in the gospels are relatively brief. It isn't hard to imagine that the resurrection could have been staged. Are the stories of the angels at the tomb, the appearances to Mary Magdalene and the Apostles of the resurrected Jesus just Christian folklore?

Almost every Christian scholar will agree that our entire faith hinges on the Resurrection of Jesus. Without that, Jesus would have been just another prophet or teacher, not the Son of God, the Savior that died for our sins. As Jesus conquered death, all of us who believe in Him will share in His victory and have the hope of sharing eternal life with Him.

So what is it that leads us to accept that the Resurrection was real? For me, it is the rapid and miraculous change in the demeanor and attitude of the Apostles. How quickly they went from being silent, fearful, and hopeless to publicly and boldly declaring the risen Jesus as Savior of the world! Something on a grand scale had to have transpired, leading to this momentous change of heart. The Acts of the Apostles records the appearances of Jesus to the Apostles after His death. We also read there the fulfillment of the promise He made in sending them (and us) the Holy Spirit and with that the gifts of the Spirit: Wisdom, Fortitude, Understanding, Counsel, Knowledge, Piety, and Fear of the Lord.

As I write this chapter of the book, it is (by God's will; I suspect) the Easter season of 2020. During the worldwide COVID-19 outbreak, for the first time in recent history, there are no Holy Week or Easter services in our churches. Much like the Apostles immediately after the death of Jesus, we are now living in solitude, fear, and anxiety. It's time to look forward and find hope and courage in the risen Jesus.

In conclusion, let us make a commitment together to take the time to **read and meditate on the Word of God and make it a priority to discover and execute God's plan for our life.** We must foster an urgency to 'tune out' the loud voices that are screaming at us from the world today and listen to what God has to say through His Word and His teachers. If you are looking for an avenue to get you started, pay a visit to the 'Bible Study' blog pages of our website, www.voicesoflaity.org. Once enlightened with His Word and Spirit, we must, as the Apostles did, become missionaries for Christ, giving testimony, preparing ourselves and others for His second coming.

VIII

MISSIONARIES FOR CHRIST

"But you will receive power when the Holy Spirit has come upon you and you shall be My witnesses both in Jerusalem, and in all Judea and Samaria, and even to 'the remotest part of the earth'."
Acts 1:8

The uncle of one of my classmates in grammar school was a Franciscan (if my memory serves me) missionary priest in Haiti. He would come as a guest to our parish twice a year to update us on the progress of his mission. Each time he came, there would be a 'second collection' to provide financial support for bringing the message of Jesus to the people of Haiti. We would listen to him tell stories about the poverty and suffering endured by the Haitians. It always amazed me at how someone could sacrifice their whole lives, surrender almost all earthly possessions, and go to a foreign country to teach people about Jesus. As a youngster, it was always hard to visualize what were their motivations and rewards?

Usually, when one thinks of being a missionary, it involves preaching the Word in a foreign country, interacting with local populations. We, as Christians and Catholics, are all called to be missionaries for Christ, summoned to spread the Good News of God's abundant grace. Called to duty in unfolding the message of Christ crucified for our sins, salvation through faith, and eternal life won for believers through His resurrection (Mark 16:15; Matt 28:19-20; Rom 10:14). So where then are our 'mission fields?' Does God expect everyone to travel to a foreign land to preach?

The reality is we don't have to go very far beyond our neighborhoods, local churches, places of employment, and even our own family and friends. It is not a significant challenge to find the 'mission fields' that desperately need the sowing of the seeds of God's true Word and grace. Each of us has within our own circle of friends and family a unique group of people to minister to that perhaps no one else may ever touch with God's message. Do you have friends, family, neighbors, and/or co-workers that have turned their back on and abandoned God altogether? Are they living an obviously sinful life with literally no consideration for the things of God? Have they become lackadaisical in their faith, led to believe 'all go to Heaven,' and feel exempt from the eternal judgment of those that die in sin and ignorance of God? Are they focused on the things of this world or the next? Is there a better place for anyone to start their missionary work than among those they love and care for the most?

The past several chapters expressed our concerns about taking the important steps in reconciling ourselves to God through examination, discernment, and repentance. These undertakings go 'hand-in-hand' with adopting a 'listening spirit', grounding ourselves in His Word, and accepting the doctrine of 'salvation by faith.'

These tasks, in themselves, are formidable, requiring a lifelong commitment. However, as we become more mature in our faith, God's additional challenge to us is to bear on our shoulders the mission of spreading our faith to others.

If you can muster the courage with the guidance of the Holy Spirit to begin your mission, we caution you regarding the various levels of resistance you may encounter. You will be up against a relentless barrage of media from around the world, working so hard to keep God and His Word out of hearts and minds.

VIII MISSIONARIES FOR CHRIST

Even now, Facebook ™ and Twitter ™ are banning and deleting more and more posts that have religious connotations or are supportive of God's Word. How hard must we labor to reach the younger generations of Catholics/Christians? When accepting God's mission know that there will be a direct relationship between how close a person is to you and the resolve required to bring up the subjects of faith, repentance, and reconciling to God. Often you will have to carefully plot your strategy incorporating a great balancing act between forcefulness and subtleness.

On the lighter side, you will find the more you seek and develop your relationship with God and experience His blessings, the more motivation you will have to share God's message with those around you. When reaching out to your fellow Catholics/Christians, it is important to understand that none of us is capable of 'saving' a lost person. They are saved only through the grace of God and an individual's acceptance of the Blood of the crucified Christ as payment for their sins. We need only be messengers, servants of God, vehicles of the Holy Spirit, convincing one and all to devote the time necessary to perpetually rebuild their relationship with God (Heb 1:14; Eph 2:8-10; Rom 11:6).

A question I've asked myself many times in the past is: 'If you think things are so bad in the Catholic Church, why not just leave the Church and join another denomination more to your liking?' It is a question I've considered, prayed on, and have continued to pray on over the past 35 years.

During the years of what I mentioned before as my 'spiritual awakening,' when I feel I was truly 'saved,' I was in my early 30s. It was during this period that I first contemplated leaving the Church and joining a more enthusiastic, evangelizing, and bible-oriented denomination. This surely would have simplified things and resulted in the 'easy way out' for me and my family. But then an amazing thing happened. The more I prayed on this, the more Jesus spoke to my heart through the Holy Spirit, enlightening and encouraging me to share instead the wonderful lessons, spiritual gifts, and blessings God bestowed on me with the Catholic community I was already part of. Repeatedly, the question I heard from the Holy Spirit was: 'Who was in more dire need of this missionary work?'

It didn't take long for me to follow God's direction and become fully immersed in many functions of my parish's operations. It was a huge transition from being a 'common' parishioner, essentially 'missing in action,' to actively taking part in an array of Church ministries.

Sharing the message of salvation through faith in Christ crucified for our sins and His resurrection had become (and still is) a major priority in my life. Announcing and showing to my fellow Catholics through the Scriptures that salvation was not something earned by 'being good' developed into my newest and biggest challenge.

Depending on which ministries you choose to become involved in, proclaiming the Word of God to your fellow parishioners is always a great place to start. As stated before, there is probably no greater need than communicating the message of salvation to both existing and ex-Catholics. Once you make a commitment to God and yourself to spread His message in your parish community, it will amaze you the impact this has on your family and close friends. Leading by example sends a profound message to all those who witness your work, shining for them a light in the darkness.

Just getting started in your missionary work can present its own set of challenges. A great first step is to set goals for identifying, evaluating, and **using your gifts and talents** to help fulfill Christ's mission. Transfigure yourselves, your mindset, your habits and routines, and meditate on the Word of God. Ask God to guide you in the direction He wants you to go and then, most importantly, **listen to Him for an answer**. Believe me, once you commit yourself to your mission, He will provide you with ample opportunities to serve Him. Be on the alert to the guidance of the Holy Spirit, who will give you opportunity, courage, and direction.

'Isn't it the job of the priests and clergy to do all this?' This is a logical question one might ask, but let's consider a 2018 Gallup poll (Saad, 2018) that shows less than 40% of overall Catholics attended weekly Mass in the

VIII MISSIONARIES FOR CHRIST

years 2014-2017 compared to 75% in 1955. Even more troubling is the decline of younger people attending services. The same poll shows a decline from 73% attendance in 1955 to 25% in 2017 for the 21-29 age group.

Looking at an even more recent Gallup Poll (Jones, 2021) in 2021 found that only 47% of Americans reported belonging to a church, synagogue, or mosque. This percentage was down from 70% just over 20 years ago in 1999. One of the key findings in this poll was the percentage of decline in church affiliation of Catholics from 76% in 1998-2000, to 58% in 2018-2020 for a total falloff of -18%. Protestants during the same timeframe suffered a loss of about half that coming in at only -9% (73% vs. 64%). This, as you might imagine, does not bode well for the future of the Church. So as the general Catholic population has progressively less and less contact with the Church and their priests, we, as laity, must take up the role as missionaries to deliver God's message. Being complacent and doing nothing risks the souls of those we know and love, falling prey to worldly desires, the Devil's lies, and ultimately eternal torment and punishment.

We don't have to dig deep to uncover reasons for declining church attendance. The clergy child abuse scandals and cover-ups of Church leadership, combined with clergy sexual immorality, complacency, greed, and laziness, can all be suggested as contributing factors. What can we expect in the 'post-COVID' era for church attendance? Certainly, we shouldn't expect an increase in Mass attendance after being absolved from the requirement during the pandemic.

The new Papal encyclical released in October 2020, Fratelli Tutti (Brother's All) (Francis, 2020), makes no suggestion of a call for Catholics to an era of repentance and renewal to Christ. Instead, we see something quite to the contrary. It is a call for humankind to come together as 'one' under the guise of 'global unity.' It reads more like an introduction and gateway towards Catholic participation in the 'New World Order.'

No longer will the conversion of souls to Christ from those in non-Christian religions be a priority. The sacrifice of the Cross will become further diminished in the eyes of the world, replaced with the doctrine of simply choosing an individual path to the eternal reward guaranteed everyone.

In conclusion, I view the biggest dynamic for the absence of enthusiasm in the Church is the lack of one gift of the Spirit, 'Fear of the Lord.' The scripture tells us that 'Fear of the Lord' is the beginning of Wisdom (Prov 9:10; 8:11-16). We must emphasize to all Christians/Catholics there will be a price to pay for those that do not recognize God's justice, ignore His Word, or lack the fear of His judgment.

Before moving on to the next few chapters, let's take a moment and reflect on the recommendations made in Part I that will help guide us on our quest for sainthood.

First, we should, as individuals, with God's help, make an honest and thorough examination of conscience and faith.

Acknowledge that, as Jesus and the Apostles taught us, the world is not intended to be our actual home (John 14:23; 1 John 2:15-17), but the road we must travel to our heavenly home is difficult, paved with many obstacles that only a very few pursue vigorously. All will be judged and **only those that have put God first above all earthly things will experience eternal reward.** It is so important that we take the time to listen to God through reading the Bible, prayer, opening our hearts to the wisdom and power of the Holy Spirit, and recognizing God's presence in our daily circumstances.

Once we have reconciled and reconnected our hearts, minds, and souls to God, we will experience His endless blessings. Nothing can be more important to us than sharing the joy of these blessings and the Good News of the death and resurrection of Jesus Christ to all of those around us, especially to our family and those we love and hold dear to our hearts.

IX

THE HYBRID CATHOLIC

"For I long to see you so that I may impart some spiritual gift to you that you may be established; that is, that I may be encouraged together with you, while among you, each of us by the other's faith, both yours and mine."
Romans 1:11-12

One of our parish Deacons was giving the sermon on a Sunday morning concerning 'Being Catholic.' Instead of speaking from the heart, he was reading the sermon 'word for word' from a script he had put down on paper, or perhaps copied from another author. Not sure why, but this method of delivery has always annoyed me to no end. It just lacks spiritual impact compared to a sermon you know is coming from the preacher's heart and soul. There was one statement he made that caught my attention: 'To be a Catholic it is all or nothing.' In the words that followed, his premise was that you must accept every doctrine and teaching of the Church to qualify as a true Catholic. For many, this philosophy may hold true, but in my opinion, it is an absurd argument. Consider the many opposing points of view and positions of ordained bishops and cardinals debating the Church's official stance on any subject or doctrine discussed in past and present formal Church Councils. There is hardly ever a unanimous consensus. Look no further than the huge policy divides existing in the Church today between traditionalists and the 'new age' ideas of Pope Francis. Take even the simple case of whether the celebration of the Latin Mass should be allowed. We certainly can't expect total agreement in views on policy, even with more prominent subject matters within the Church, like changes made during Vatican II.

'Cafeteria Catholic' is a common term used today identifying individuals that 'pick and choose' certain Catholic doctrine to follow but not others. Do you acknowledge the Trinity but not the Church's stated obligation to attend Mass every week? Believe in Heaven and Hell, but not Purgatory? I'm sorry, you are not a full-fledged Catholic. How dare we debate the doctrines and policies of our perfect Church and its infallible leaders? Some will call it heresy to question Catholic dogma, even if these doctrines are more related to 'tradition' with only loosely substantiated ties to the Bible.

This chapter, I pray, helps to explain how the amazing spiritual lessons absorbed from outside the Church, combined with my lifelong inherited Catholic doctrines, have shaped me into what I call a 'Hybrid Catholic.' It is my sincere hope by sharing these experiences with you, they can also help **contribute to the growth in your faith.**

The impact of the teachings from outside of the Church has played such an important role in my spiritual development. I truly believe I would not have gained my salvation without them. A key goal of mine in writing this book was to bring to light these principles and beliefs for anyone willing to take the time to listen and act on them, but especially for Catholics who may have never heard these vital messages regarding God's plan for our salvation. You will have to make a choice to agree or disagree with these basic points and I hope that through your prayers and enlightenment from the Holy Spirit, it will inspire you to come to the right conclusions.

You may ask, why can't we just follow the rules of the Church and be happily on our way to heaven? It should be obvious to most, especially those still going to church regularly, that this path is just not working. I've labored in the faith for many years, monitoring the beliefs and attitudes of my fellow Catholics. My experiences have led me to grave concerns for

IX THE HYBRID CATHOLIC

much of the Catholic faithful. For a long time now, they've been lulled into a dangerous realm of spiritual complacency. There are so many who are naïve toward the true teachings of the Word and message of salvation by faith, and so few that have the fervor to pursue, renew, and grow their relationship with God. Countless Catholics are content to remain on a spiritual level much lower than what they can truly achieve. Some are at the level where you might question their salvation.

It is easy for me to relate to this mindset, having lived through many years of this false sense of satisfaction and spiritual security. Absent of a receptive heart and mind to the Word, my relationship with God would not have grown into what it has become today. There's a good chance I would have been destined to eternal punishment for my failure to make God the priority in my life. Instead, having grown and developed into this 'Hybrid Catholic' state, I feel spiritually fulfilled with the blessings of God our Father, and the gifts of the Holy Spirit. All granted to me through the saving graces of Our Lord Jesus Christ.

There have been many groups victimized by the recent demise of the Church. The most prominent, I think we all would agree, are the children and families affected by the clergy sex abuse scandals. Next in line are those in religious communities subjected unwillingly, most times, to the sexual advances of their peers and superiors. But on an even grander scale, we can point to one group tremendously affected by the Church crises having gone relatively unnoticed, or even identified as victims. These are the thousands of loyal and dedicated Catholic priests, bishops, nuns, and lay ministers who do amazing work every day to bring Christ's message to the faithful. For their efforts, many are now being 'canceled' and/or having their work diminished by the actions of the Church hierarchy in the Vatican. Lucky enough to have a faithful and dedicated pastor in my current parish, I have a deeply rooted sense that he holds back on saying and preaching what he truly believes in fear of reprimand by the local Bishop. It would certainly be of no surprise to me if this holds true for many of the dedicated clergy.

For most organizations, the lack of trust in the morality and ethics of the establishment's highest leadership eventually trickles down to the 'rank and file' within such an entity. If the policies advanced from a corrupt Church hierarchy influence the messages we receive as Catholics from the pulpit on Sundays, how then are we able to absorb the key truths and inspirations of the Holy Spirit? Can we effectively discern and spread the genuine message of salvation? The solution lies in the ability to keep our minds, hearts, and souls open to extending our relationship with God through accessing the best resources existing both inside and outside of the Church. While the internet and social media in particular, are sometimes identified as key contributors to the moral decay of our society, these outlets can also serve us with wonderful tools in bringing us closer to God. Christian television shows, YouTube ™ videos, Facebook ™and Twitter™ pages, podcasts, and religious web sites are all examples of digital destinations capable of enabling and enhancing our spiritual growth.

Referencing many of the 'cyber locations' and media that have helped me on my faith journey in this book, I hope you take the time to inspect these and, through your research, find new and exciting sites you can share with me and others. You can expand your spiritual horizons without giving up the Catholic beliefs we know and hold so dearly in our hearts. However, there is one thing we must always keep foremost in our minds about exploring these opportunities. As we set out to expand our knowledge and grow ourselves spiritually, remember the importance of **measuring the worth and validity of whatever doctrines and messages we may discover against what is revealed to us in the Word of God and the Laws He has written in our hearts.**

If you come across an interesting subject or a media site, please share it with us at www.voicesoflaity.org. A visit to the 'Resources' page of our website will give you a list of 'vetted' sites of interest to get you started. These venues are from both inside and outside the Catholic faith.

X
LOVE, LOVE, LOVE

"Be on the alert, stand firm in the faith, act like men, be strong. Let all that you do be done in love."
1 Corinthians 16:13-14

It would be difficult to find a word in the English language that can encompass so many meanings, emotions, and reflections than the word 'love.' The love we have for our immediate family, our brothers, sisters, and parents tends, mostly, to differ from the love we share with our spouse, partner, and/or children. We also hear people relate a feeling of love toward their favorite sports teams, foods, wines, cars, games, etc. There are just so many examples of how we use this word in our everyday lives.

I have been fortunate enough to share my love with the same person for over 50 years. Having met her during the summer after my senior year of high school, we married four years later. In June 2020, we celebrated our 50th year together, 46th married. She has always been my 'rock,' the foundation on which we have built a wonderful family and both our physical and spiritual lives. Teaching me about love has probably been her greatest gift, and through her example of faith lives a joyful, selfless life sharing these attributes with all she comes in contact with.

For those of you that have had a genuine experience of 'falling in love,' you understand the impact this can have on your heart, mind, and soul. In the initial stages of the relationship, while developing a mutual love, you can focus on almost nothing else. You are constantly thinking about that person anxiously waiting for the next opportunity to meet up with and/or speak with them. You will sacrifice the time spent with other friends or your 'normal' routines to be with them. The time you spend together is typically joyful and full of happiness. It is an intense and wonderful feeling that you hope will be enduring.

As great as this feeling can be, the chances are good that these emotions become fleeting as the relationship progresses over the months and years. The 'spark' that ignited the fire so brightly in the beginning seems to diminish as time goes by and the connection slowly grows stale. Before you know it, each person in the relationship takes the other for granted, becomes bored, and eventually lacks the inspiration needed to rekindle what once was a flourishing bond.

The Bible tells us that God is love (1 John 4: 7-19; Rom 8:37-39). God loves his creation and all of us in it. He loves every one of us, sinners and saints, with an everlasting love that does not fade away. He calls us all to be His own and to reciprocate this same love towards Him and our fellow man. It is so important that we not hold back our love toward anyone because they differ from us or have views that are inconsistent with our own. Race, religion, creed, gender, sexual orientation, political persuasion, etc. cannot factor in determining who we should or should not offer our love and support to. Jesus, the living Word of God, profoundly preached this same gospel of love to all. We should, through our living example, continue the message of Christ to remove all hatred from our hearts and the hearts of all the men and women we come in contact with.

Just as we come to know and love a person when building a human relationship, so it must be with God. Like that of a child to a parent, we must know it is only those willing to commit to and maintain a close personal relationship with Him that will receive the eternal reward He has promised and prepared for His children. Satan wants our souls for his own when we

X LOVE, LOVE, LOVE

pass from this world and will do anything to keep us from establishing ourselves into the family of God and being welcomed into His eternal home. I can't imagine how fiercely angry the Devil must be at God who would allow us, mere humans, to share in His heavenly home. This while Lucifer and the fallen angels, once regarded in such high stature, are banned eternally from heaven.

The Word of God tells us He wants all to be saved through the blood of His Son, Jesus Christ, but very few are willing to actively pursue His promises. Can you imagine knocking on a stranger's door and asking or expecting them to allow you to come live with them if they didn't know you? Of course, you wouldn't. We should then accept that this holds true and applies to God and His magnificent home in Heaven. I've noted this before, but it bears repeating. Realize that God does not exclude us from Heaven or 'send us to hell.' It is not by God's choice but by **the choices we make** that ultimately influence our eternal destiny. If we choose to live our life here on earth absent from God, so then our bodies and spirits will be eternally separated from Him in the fires of Hell when we die.

In getting to know, love, and serve God, we need to ask ourselves: Is there a hunger in our hearts to come to know and love Him? Are we willing to sacrifice earthly distractions to build this relationship? Any commitment we make to a relationship requires time. How much of our time are we willing to give to God?

There are no substitutes for prayer along with reading and meditating on the Word of God to bring us to the point of establishing a genuine connection to God the Father through Jesus and the Holy Spirit. You would probably agree that the most successful interactions happen when the parties involved not only hear what the others are saying, but actively listen to them. In our prayers, we must take the time to 'actively' listen to the convictions of the Holy Spirit and the paths we need to follow in changing our lives to one that is in a constant state of discernment and repentance. Continuous communication with God is the key to a successful and joyful prayer life.

From my own experiences, I can testify to the difficulty you may endure sustaining the excitement of your newly found connection with and love for God. Without going into the details (which would take another book), with the help of God, I worked through and eventually overcame fierce demonic attacks after recommitting myself to God. This brought me to the place where I am today, enjoying Christ's peace in my heart while engaged in a fulfilling connection with the Holy Spirit, inspiring me to share the gospel message.

You should not be surprised if you observe parallels between your spiritual love relationship with God and what you may have encountered in your human endeavors. When I first realized the genuine message of salvation by faith, it was so easy to be 'on fire with the Holy Spirit.' As previously mentioned, I became involved in so many ministries at my church and just couldn't help giving of myself to bring the message of Christ crucified to my fellow parishioners. For those of you reading this book and are possibly for the first time coming to this same enlightenment through the Holy Spirit, you may experience a similar type of euphoria. But just as with human relationships, you must guard against this connection growing stale. Be warned, this state of mind can be fragile and subject to intense attack from the Devil. Satan does not just throw his hands in the air and say, 'oh well, there's one soul I lost.' His attacks on you and levels of temptations will increase. He will do all in his power to entice you back to your previous lifestyle, tarnish and diminish your testimony, and limit your effectiveness in sharing the gospel with others.

So let us now go forth to love God and one another as we wait in joyful hope for the coming of our Savior, Jesus Christ.

PART ONE CONCLUSION

"Therefore, having these promises, beloved, let us cleanse ourselves from all defilement of flesh and spirit, perfecting holiness in the fear of God."
2 Corinthians 7:1

It is my hope you have taken to heart some steps suggested here in Part I to help guide you on your quest for 'sainthood.' The primary motivation behind authoring this manuscript was to share my beliefs and experiences with the hope they might inspire fellow Catholics/Christians into a renewal of their faith. This rekindling of faith can become for us a pillar of support as we brace ourselves and prepare for the imminent coming of His judgment on our country and the world. As bad as recent world events have been, we can expect the worst is still to come. The refusal to repent from our worship of the idols of this world brought forth through Satan will slowly bring about the destruction of the way of life as we know it.

The signs of evil in the world today point toward the need to place an emphasis on committing to a life of holiness and surrendering ourselves by giving over our lives to the love and protection of the true living God. While each of us must find our path to salvation and sainthood, I humbly submit Part I of this book as a blueprint in providing some guidance to dedicating ourselves to this undertaking.

Our denial in acknowledging God as One who built our country to its greatness based on His Godly principles will ultimately have its consequences. As foretold in the Scriptures, the 'New World Order' with the encouragement and consent of the Catholic Church may very well be unfolding before our eyes and with it the impending persecution of those who hold fast to the genuine Christian faith. We must pray to the Holy Spirit for the wisdom and courage to remain loyal servants of Our Lord Jesus Christ and together face the challenge of enduring in our faith. It is time for us to 'put on the full armor of God so that we may stand firm against the schemes of the Devil... taking up the shield of faith... the helmet of salvation... and the sword of the Spirit, which is the Word of God (Eph 6:10-17).'

PART TWO
LOST KEYS TO THE KINGDOM

XI

WHO LEFT THE DOOR UNLOCKED?

"I know that you are neither cold nor hot; I wish that you were cold or hot. So because you are lukewarm, and neither hot nor cold, I will spit you out from My mouth. (God's message to the church in Laodecia)"
Revelations 3:15-16

Being a practicing Catholic in today's world certainly can be challenging. Born and raised in the Catholic faith, I believe it to be my destiny and God's will that I die a Catholic (not necessarily Roman Catholic). I joke with my family I must first assume that excommunication will not be my fate for writing this manuscript. In Part II of this book, I hope to relay and describe my feelings on where the Catholic Church stands today in this rapidly changing, complex world. Undoubtedly, each of you has your thoughts and opinions on where the Church is positioned, and your views certainly may be quite contrary to mine.

It is time to set the scene of why it is so important for us, as Catholic laity, to rise, be heard, and become so much more involved in the spreading of the Gospel. To do this, a first step is making a disturbingly difficult but honest evaluation of the Catholic Church. We must consider its complacency in delivering God's message to the faithful, and the current depraved condition of its leadership. When speaking with fellow Catholics, I have observed many who purposely choose to remain blind to the truth, unwilling to investigate, admit, comprehend, or digest the extent of these serious problems. The litany of issues confronting the Church are 'swept under the rug' so their lives can go on without interruption, the way it always has. These attitudes, adopted by a good percentage of the laity, only contribute to and expand the effects generated from the complacency and cover-ups exercised by Church leadership.

There is an array of subject matter to discuss regarding the present condition of the Catholic Church. Starting on a positive note, a great deal of what's going on in the Church can be considered constructive, and I would imagine very pleasing to God. There are countless numbers of Catholic priests, bishops, clergy, nuns, and laity that are spiritually committed to Our Lord Jesus Christ and do wonderful works throughout the world every day. I believe if we could count the acts of charity and mercy performed each day, Catholics would lead the way by a wide margin over any other faith. Just the sheer number of Catholics in the world says something. They carry these works and acts of charity out despite the apostasy and hypocrisy displayed by Church leadership.

I'm sure many (especially older readers) long for the ways things were in the Church during their youth. Having grown up in the era of the late 1950s and '60s, my recollection is of pews being filled to capacity with parishioners of all ages. You could feel and almost touch the spirit of Christ in our midst. We considered the Mass an 'event' with, believe it or not, four altar boys at High Mass. As a youngster, serving at Mass was always a great thrill for me, especially if I got to serve in the capacity of emcee. Yes, back then there was a certain 'mystique' and reverence associated with the liturgy of the Latin Mass. It was almost a necessity to follow along in your St. Joseph's missal to get the English translations as the priest recited the Mass prayers. They required altar boys to memorize the Mass prayers in Latin,

XI WHO LEFT THE DOOR UNLOCKED?

and I still remember many of them to this day. These are all such fond memories.

Despite all the good that is being done, today our Church faces the greatest challenges in its history. Honestly and regrettably, I don't hold out much hope for overcoming the self-inflicted obstacles it has created in these trying and turbulent times. Maintaining the long-term sustainability of the Catholic Church would be a monumental task, even if there was a willingness and ability by leadership to undertake the changes necessary to accomplish this. While I wish this was not the case, from my point of view, we are well past the 'point of no return.' The calamities now plaguing the Papacy and Church leaders in Rome have resulted from reformed Church doctrine and policies that conformed to the 'changing world' rather than trying to change the world to conform to the will of God. These include many of the doctrines put forward by the Church because of Vatican II. High-level Freemason clergy infiltrators strongly influenced the Vatican II final doctrines, according to Dr. Taylor Marshall in his previously mentioned book, *'Infiltration.'* These altered doctrines and guidelines, some of which I believe run in direct contrast to the Word of God, developed over the years into a series of failed and desperate measures employed by Church leaders to slow down the continuing exodus of faithful Catholics. It should, however, come as no surprise to us when observing the effects and considering the origins of these ideologies that they continue to backfire, resulting in quite the opposite outcomes.

Many would say that looking back through the centuries of Church history, it has been in much more difficult situations. I tend to disagree. With the advent of the internet and the proliferation of worldwide mainstream and social media, the veil of secrecy that has protected the Church from ultimate scrutiny and transparency throughout the ages has now been lifted. The 'Revelation' is at hand.

If you thought St. Paul was angry with the early Christian faithful in Galatia for following the teachings of the Judaizers in his letter to the Galatians

(Gal 1:6-10), what would he say/write now if he were to visit the present-day Church of Rome? He would find a Church leadership filled with greed, laziness, complacency to obvious sexual sin, and openly bearing satanic symbols and imagery. A Church that has amassed countless riches on the backs of poor Catholics throughout the ages.

When discerning recorded 'visions' or prophecies by living persons, including popes and saints, it has always been my policy to take each of these with at least a 'small grain of salt.' That being said, I recently came across the story of a vision of Pope Leo XIII, which I feel connects with our narrative above and the current day situation, which I'd like to share.

This vision reportedly came to him immediately after saying Mass, falling into a trance and collapsing to the ground in October 1884. There were only a handful of people, mostly clergy, attending daily Mass in the Pope's chapel to record this event. He later relayed his vision to the others that were present. It was that of Satan standing before the throne of Jesus boasting that he could destroy the Church if given a 100-year period, where he was to have more power over those that serve him. Jesus replied that the true Church will never be destroyed and exist until the end of time, but Jesus granted the request of Satan for 100 years. Further visions into the next century revealed to Pope Leo were great wars (WWI & WWII?), increases in immorality, homosexuality, and mass genocides. A look at the state of our world today reveals these events have, mostly, come to fruition, including the genocide of the Jews in occupied Europe by the Nazis, Ukrainians by the Russians, and the legalized abortions in our modern societies. Another vision of Pope Leo revealed demons sitting on the throne of the Papacy. Could that be the case in Rome today?

Pope Leo then authored the prayer to Michael the Archangel, which a few years later was recited at the end of each low Mass. This prayer was later suppressed by one of the Vatican II documents, *Inter oecumenici*, in 1965 and more recently by Pope Francis.

XI WHO LEFT THE DOOR UNLOCKED?

I wish there was some scenario I could envision that would provide hope for the reversal of this downward spiral. Frankly, I just don't see it. Perhaps some of my readers could enlighten and encourage me with a solution, relieving me of this despair? Are the visions of Pope Leo and Satan's claims coming to fulfillment? Are we at or near the end of the 100 years? Who left the door unlocked to let the demons in?

Was it just coincidence that lightning struck twice at the Vatican just hours after the resignation of Pope Benedict (BBC, 2013)? Along with the impact of major current events such as the resignation of Pope Benedict XVI and the defrocking of Washington DC Cardinal McCarrick, many recently published articles and books finally shed some light on those truths hidden, or perhaps intentionally overlooked by the laity and church leaders for many years. Just recently (Nov. 2020), the Vatican finally released their investigative report on the disturbing activities of Cardinal McCarrick. Probably one of the most ominous findings of the report was that Pope (or should I say Saint?) John Paul II was well aware of McCarrick's homosexual lifestyle and antics before 'promoting' him to Cardinal (Neuman, 2020).

More current headlines tell us that half of New York State's eight Catholic dioceses have now filed for bankruptcy because of paying claims to sexual abuse victims, with more dioceses and religious orders doing the same (Wolf, 2021). All of this, while the Vatican is embroiled in yet another (Oct. 2020) financial scandal involving millions of euros for real estate investments and alleged money laundering for the mafia. As a result, it has forced Cardinal Becciu to resign with even more ramifications expected coming down the pike. Vatican operatives have reportedly embezzled even the Pope's own 'discretionary fund' (20M Euros).

During my research, one book stood out to me in defining the ongoing betrayal of the clergy to the Catholic faithful, the gospel of Christ, and His Church. It is a publication I encourage every Catholic to read titled *'The Smoke of Satan - How Corrupt and Cowardly Bishops Betrayed Christ, His Church and the Faithful... and What Can Be Done About It'* by Philip

Lawler, (Lawler, 2018). Mr. Lawler is an author and journalist who has been covering Catholicism for over 30 years. He is the founder of Catholic World News and news director and lead analyst for CatholicCulture.org. In this book, he paints a fascinating picture of the comfort and complacency of the Church's clergy built up over decades. He reveals how through parish pulpits these attitudes have since translated to the faithful, resulting in a steady decline of active members in the Catholic Church. The content affirms while major declarations from the Vatican and Bishop's Councils support standard Catholic doctrines on things like abortion, homosexuality, divorce, etc., local bishops, pastors, and priests are afraid to preach on or enforce these issues for fear of political and social backlash from parishioners and society.

In summary, the Catholic clergy, including the leadership, are not practicing what the Church preaches. While all this may paint a depressing picture, some hope shines through. It comes from the author's vision in 'Smoke of Satan' for the laity to rise, evangelize, and make the valiant effort required to renew the Church. *'Last Call to Sainthood'* and the Voices of Catholic Laity (VOCAL) Ministries (www.voicesoflaity.org) website are my humble contributions to this effort.

XII

SEXUAL SIN, THE CHURCH AND REPENTANCE

"For this is the will of God, your sanctification; that is, that you abstain from sexual immorality, that each of you know how to possess his own vessel in sanctification and honor, not in lustful passions..."
1 Thessalonians 4:3-4

Perhaps it is time for all of us to rejoice because over the past 60 years God has finally come to his senses and has eliminated adultery, fornication, homosexuality, divorce, and sodomy from those actions that are considered sins and offensive to Him. Even better than that, we now know that everyone goes to heaven! Unless, of course, you are an unrepentant serial rapist or murderer, but even then you have a chance. There is no need for us to go to Mass, receive the Eucharist, repent from our sins, or contribute to our local parishes. 'Fear of God' has become an obsolete concept, because after all, what is there to fear? He is a 'loving God' and forgives **everyone**, no problem. Surely He is not mean enough to send anyone to Hell. Why would He? We aren't doing anything wrong. Just make sure you are baptized, lead a life of goodwill and you're guaranteed a spot in heaven.

How many of you, when reading the paragraph above, believed in the sincerity of these words or knew I meant them to be 'tongue in cheek?' You may not be willing to admit it, but the ideologies presented in the paragraph above are among one of the more prevailing sentiments and philosophies practiced by Catholics and other Christians in our society today. What is most disturbing, if you consider it, this is exactly the way the Devil would like you to think. Aligning your spirit with this kind of messaging means Satan has completed his work and need not waste any more of his time and effort. He's got you.

It is amazing to me how much we underestimate the power of Satan in the world today, despite the evidence of his reign over a vast number of the world's population. We're deceived into thinking that because a significant event or a dictated policy is attributed to a Christian church (including the Catholic Church), then it must surely be from God. We come to accept these things without discernment, even though they may be in direct conflict with the Word of God. Remember St. Paul in his letter to the Corinthians tells us that Satan will masquerade himself as an 'angel of light' (2 Cor 11:13-15). For obvious reasons, he will not show himself as who he really is. So what may appear as truths coming from the mouths of the righteous, or even apparent apparitions or miracles, might actually be the lies and exercised powers of the Devil. Our one true 'measuring stick' in discerning whether any spiritual events or teachings are true or false has to be the Word of God, the Bible, and not the opinions of human endeavors.

Victories won and enjoyed by the Devil in pursuit of human souls can and will quickly become squandered through repentance of sins and trust in the saving sacrifice of Jesus on the cross as payment for them. It is only then that the Devil will have to toil to win back your soul.

Over the past several years of my faith journey, repentance has consistently been a top priority. Putting ourselves and the things of this world above God every day in disobedience is so easy to do. It leads us into the trap of becoming complacent in our repentance. As we engage in the early stages

XII SEXUAL SIN, THE CHURCH AND REPENTANCE

of our confession and repentance, there can exist in us a great feeling of triumph and euphoria. Don't expect that Lucifer will just give up on you. You can expect just the opposite. As mentioned previously, anticipate, as you enter a state of repentance, his attacks and temptations leading you back to sin will become more ferocious than ever. The last thing he wants is for you to escape his deadly grasp.

Before continuing, I want to clarify that this chapter deals with sexual sin and how it has permeated and affected the Catholic Church. It is not the intent of this book to 'gay bash,' clergy bash, or to judge anyone. There should be zero tolerance of fear, hatred, or violence toward anyone, regardless of their gender, race, ethnicity, religion, sexual orientation, or beliefs. Jesus taught us to love, pray for, and respect everyone in God's creation, even more so those who may have opposing views to our own. (John 4: 1-42; John 8: 1-11) This is something sorely needed in the world today.

I have both friends and relatives in the LGBTQ community that I love and pray for. In reciprocation, I also feel their love towards me. Like it or not, **God is pro-choice**, giving us probably the greatest gift in all His Creation, the free will to live our lives as we desire. He will judge us all on how we exercised our gift of free will based first on the measure of our love, faith, and obedience to Him, and second, on the love we show to our neighbors. Always keep in mind that **God is love**.

I believe that if you are part of the LGBTQ community and have a close personal relationship with God; you don't need me or anyone else blasting scripture verses at you that may pertain to God's disapproval and/or rejection of your lifestyle. You would know well these biblical references, and through your prayer have believed that they are no longer binding. If you do not have a close personal relationship with God, then your sexual orientation is irrelevant regarding His judgement.

The temptation to commit sexual sin and act on lustful desires affects nearly every one of us in our lives, and I am certainly no exception to this. Having acted myself on the Devil's temptations, I can attest to the difficulty that arises in breaking with the addictive nature of these sinful habits. As with most sin, whether it be gluttony, greed, sloth, etc., lust and sexual sin result from pride and putting our satisfaction and glory above God's. There are too many New and Old Testament verses on sexual purity to list them all, but you can start with these: 1 Cor 6:13-18; 2 Col 3:5; Hebrews 13:4.

My interpretation of the bible leaves me no doubt that God has defined homosexuality and sodomy as sins. While we are all sinners who need the guidance of the Holy Spirit and the welcoming of the Church, with that inclusion, there must also be a call to an examination of conscience and repentance. Jesus presented examples of this in the cases of the adulterous woman (John 8:3-11), and the Samaritan woman at the well (John 4:6-29). God also makes clear in His Holy Word that He holds us responsible and accountable for the admonishment of the sins of our fellow brothers and sisters (Thes 5:14-15; Luke 17:1-4; Ezekiel 33:18-19; Matt 12:36-37; Romans 1:18-23). If we recognize in our family, friends, or neighbors what we understand to be a blatant sinful life and stand by and say and do nothing, we will be held accountable to God. Recently I read a Facebook™ meme that said "Don't judge me because I sin differently than you." While this statement has some profound merit to it, understand we are all called to bring each other to holiness, and that tolerance of any sin should not equate to God's acceptance of the sin, diminished judgment, or prevent a call to repentance.

As we speak of admonishment, we should be clear on what Jesus taught us so that we perform it with love and encouragement, and not with hatred, bitterness, anger, and condemnation. He gives us the perfect model of this when dealing with the adulterous woman who was about to be stoned, according to Jewish law, for her sin (John 8:3-11). While He made the point of saying there was no one left to condemn her (including Him), He also clarified that she needed to change her lifestyle through repentance, saying: **'Go. From now on sin no more.'** We must all receive this same message in our hearts and then 'pay forward' this lesson to all of those around us. Each new

XII SEXUAL SIN, THE CHURCH AND REPENTANCE

day presents us with opportunities to examine our conscience, foster the admonishment of sins, encourage repentance in those around us, and renew the hearts of our brothers and sisters to Our Lord Jesus Christ.

While observing the prevailing attitudes towards sex in our society today, it constantly reminds us of the ever-expanding problems that persist in the Catholic Church behind (mostly) closed doors around the world.

Of course, the pedophilia issue tops the list, creating headlines since 2002. There are more than enough searchable resources out there that provide extensive details on this subject, so I feel no need to focus much on that here. This issue, supposedly addressed by the Church years ago, has seen just as recently as the summer of 2018 the headlines and saga continue. A recent summit on child sexual abuse held at the Vatican in March 2019 accomplished little.

This subject becomes even more convoluted, extending beyond the bounds of the Church. The Associated Press released a story in October 2019 (Authors, 2019) about thousands of currently defrocked and retired 'credibly accused' clergy now living amongst and working with children in various social occupational roles. Having not been formally tried and convicted as criminals, these former clergy and religious escape scrutiny by not showing up in background checks as sexual offenders. We can see from this investigative work that this could be the proverbial 'tip of the iceberg' in terms of how many former clergy out there fall into this category and continue to represent an imminent danger to the children of our society.

Another powerful secret that the Church has kept from us is the growing presence of homosexuality, sodomy, and the 'gay agenda' imbedded within the clergy that has slowly found its way into the highest levels of the Church leadership. It has affected all ranks of the Catholic hierarchy, from local seminaries to the existing chain of command at the Vatican. The implicit code of silence observed by the clergy on these issues in the past projected a giant veil of secrecy draped over the truth. Efforts to conceal these realities from the general population of Catholics are becoming more and more diminished, exposing attitudes of brazen defiance by our Church leaders. A theory presented by several critics of the Church suggests headlines brought on by the child sex abuse scandals have deflected attention from this even bigger concern crippling our Church.

Besides observing the obvious, to be convinced these trends exist, I recommend reading *'In the Closet of the Vatican—Power, Homosexuality, Hypocrisy'* by Frédéric Martel (Martel, 2019). This book provides many firsthand accounts of these phenomena from all levels of clergy and staff at the Vatican, and in countries around the world. The author is himself a gay man and this 500+ page book results from over four years of extensive research and interviews with many eye-opening revelations. While there is much to digest in this book, one of the author's major theories affirms the suggestions that the clergy's bond and commitment to secrecy concerning widespread homosexuality contributed to the concealment of the child sexual abuse and cover-up scandals that have since come to light over the past twenty years.

The author gives us what seems to be a reasonable hypothesis of how the infiltration of homosexuality into the clergy came to be. The theory is in the 1950s and 1960s in Europe and the US, there was a great stigma attached in our societies with being a homosexual male. Young homosexual men found refuge in the seminaries where they associated primarily with men, no longer questioned about their sexuality, and given a 'sense of power' in the priesthood. These priests ordained 40-50+ years ago have now worked their way up into the hierarchy as Monsignors, Bishops, and Cardinals. Some have labeled this phenomenon of the infiltration of homosexuality into the highest levels of the Vatican as **'The Lavender Mafia.'** A simple Google™ search on this topic will provide you with an array of articles written in many prestigious Catholic publications. As homosexuality and sodomy became increasingly acceptable in modern societies during the 1970s, more and more clergy began physically acting on their desires and things 'snowballed' from there. This change in our culture's attitude toward homosexu-

XII SEXUAL SIN, THE CHURCH AND REPENTANCE

ality, where there is no longer a stigma attached to being gay, among other factors, helped contribute to the precipitous decline in the enrollment of young men into the seminary.

While *'In the Closet of the Vatican'* has some 'weird spots,' and the writing can be at times very awkward and self-promoting for the author, it reveals the magnitude of these matters that should be a major concern of every Catholic.

Another media venue to explore if you'd like to dig deeper into these topics and if you are more of a 'visual' person, is to get on YouTube™ and search for Michael Voris/'Church Militant's' videos under the name 'Vortex.'

While the primary intent of this book is to encourage the forging of a renewed sense of commitment to God, I felt Catholics everywhere needed to take an honest look at how dire the situation in the Church is. We must resist turning a blind eye to its current state of affairs. An urgent call to action by the laity is required if those remaining as the Catholic faithful have any chance at all for true salvation. There is enough 'expert' material out there on these subjects to fill the pages of several books. My point of view on this web of sexual immorality the Church has fallen into is that of only a simple layperson. For a better perspective, let's look at an assessment from one of the Church's most notable leaders.

Perhaps the most interesting and damning testimony on the indictments confronting the Church, its leadership, and the current Pope (Francis) comes from Cardinal Carlo Viganò in his now-famous letter 'Testimonizia' (Testimony) dated August 22, 2018 (Vigano, 2018). It deals extensively with the abuses and subsequent cover-ups at the highest levels of the Vatican (including Pope Francis) related to Cardinal Theodore McCarrick and other high-ranking clergy. In his message, Cardinal Viganò relates to the aforementioned 'The Lavender Mafia' using the words 'homosexual current' amongst the clergy. **I implore you to follow the link in the bibliography at the end of this book and take the time to read this entire**

document. It will be valuable for you to gain the perspective of this respected Cardinal.

Here is an excerpt taken from Cardinal Viganò's 'Testimony' that I hope will motivate you to read it in its entirety (underlining is in the original text):

[Bishops and priests, abusing their authority, have committed horrendous crimes to the detriment of their faithful, minors, innocent victims, and young men eager to offer their lives to the Church, or by their silence have not prevented that such crimes continue to be perpetrated.

To restore the beauty of holiness to the face of the Bride of Christ, which is terribly disfigured by so many abominable crimes, and if we truly want to free the Church from the fetid swamp into which she has fallen, we must have the courage to tear down the culture of secrecy and publicly confess the truths we have kept hidden. We must tear down the conspiracy of silence with which bishops and priests have protected themselves at the expense of their faithful, a conspiracy of silence that in the eyes of the world risks making the Church look like a sect, a conspiracy of silence not so dissimilar from the one that prevails in the mafia. "Whatever you have said in the dark... shall be proclaimed from the housetops" (Luke 12:3).

"Now in the United States a chorus of voices is rising especially from the lay faithful, and has recently been joined by several bishops and priests, asking that all those who, by their silence, covered up McCarrick's criminal behavior, or who used him to advance their career or promote their intentions, ambitions, and power in the Church, should resign."

But this will not be enough to heal the situation of extremely grave immoral behavior by the clergy: bishops and priests. A time of conversion and penance must be proclaimed. The virtue of chastity must be recovered in the clergy and in seminaries. Corruption in the misuse of the Church's resources and of the offerings of the faithful must be fought against. The seriousness of homosexual behavior must be denounced. The homosexual networks present in the Church must be eradicated, as Janet Smith, Professor of Moral Theology at the Sacred Heart Major Seminary in Detroit, re-

XII SEXUAL SIN, THE CHURCH AND REPENTANCE

cently wrote. *"The problem of clergy abuse,"* she wrote, *"cannot be resolved simply by the resignation of some bishops, and even less so by bureaucratic directives. The deeper problem lies in homosexual networks within the clergy, which must be eradicated.* These homosexual networks, which are now widespread in many dioceses, seminaries, religious orders, etc., act under the concealment of secrecy and lies with the power of octopus tentacles, and strangle innocent victims and priestly vocations, and are strangling the entire Church."]

It is important to mention here that Cardinal Viganò is one of the few Cardinals that has had the courage to stand up against the atrocities that are going on in the Church today. More recently, he also called into question how some proposals started at Vatican II came to be confirmed as Church doctrine. Cardinal Viganò has a documented history of uncovering corruption in the Church and has paid a price for it. Some Church insiders describe him as a heretic, causing a schism in the Church. Viganò once held what they consider the third most powerful position at the Vatican, Secretary-General of the Vatican City Governorate. After discovering and reporting massive financial corruption at the Vatican (Vatican Leaks scandal), they removed him from this position and assigned him as Apostolic Nuncio to the United States. Viganò even had direct communications with President Trump warning him of the forces of evil existing in our nation (Vigano, Archbishop Vigano warns President Trump about 'Great Reset' in an Open Letter, 2020).

They estimate in some circles that conservatively over 35% of the current clergy have a homosexual orientation, with some estimations as high as 80%. These overwhelming numbers have put the Church in such an uneasy situation, making it almost impossible for leadership to take a stand on this matter. Even if it wanted to take a position with gay priests and bishops calling them to repentance, surely there would be no support from the College of Cardinals and the 'Lavender Mafia' at the Vatican. Adding to this problem, if homosexual priests and bishops left their ministries, further reducing the number of clergy, the Church would probably collapse. As an 'icing on the cake,' many would say the greatest fear facing the Church now is the potential attacks and backlash from the liberal media at the first mention of any 'anti-gay' agenda or measures.

Having raised my family in the Boston area during the tenure of Cardinal Law, the child abuse issues affected us directly. A few of the victims, belonging to the parish of my youth, were close friends of my children. Living through these experiences, it is unimaginable to me what it would be like for a member of the clergy approaching and facing the judgment throne of God having been guilty and unrepentant of these despicable acts on children, and perhaps even worse, involved in the cover-up that allowed (and continues to allow) this evil to continue.

We should expect over the next twenty years or so, a large percentage of current priests will be retired or deceased. Qualified young men willing to devote their lives to the Catholic priesthood in the service of God are getting so much harder to find. This drop in the number of clergy is forcing churches in many parts of the US to close at a rapid rate, with area parishes moving toward 'collaborative efforts,' compelled to combine resources in an environment of declining parishioner attendance. We can only expect this phenomenon to get worse. There is talk now at the Vatican that they are thinking of allowing married men to be priests, which I believe would help with the crisis. But again, we can almost be sure of opposition from those in the homosexual factions of the Church.

The trend of dwindling Catholic clergy hit home for me several years ago while my son was at seminary. I did some work for the diocese in the seminary's business office and I noticed hanging in one of the long hallways, in chronological order, were pictures of the seminary's graduating classes of ordained priests for each year. In the mid-1950s, there appeared to be 50-60 priests in each of the classes. Then, with each passing year, the numbers in the pictures progressively declined, until there were less than 10 by the early 2000s. Recently, I had a similar experience while visiting a neighboring

XII SEXUAL SIN, THE CHURCH AND REPENTANCE

church. They posted sequential pictures of the confirmation classes for each of the last 25 years in the hallway. Similarly, as the years progressed, the class sizes got significantly smaller and smaller.

There is cause for concern on many fronts. The obvious failures at the highest levels of Church leadership do not show any signs of abating. Catholics of my generation that make up the vast majority of Mass-goers are lulled into complacency with sermon after sermon designed to make everyone feel 'comfortable.' To me, it can be described as an almost 'zombie-like' devotion. Ask yourself when was the last time you heard a sermon from your local priest that caught you 'on fire with the Holy Spirit?'

Given the current state of chaos and failures of our Church leadership, I believe the last line of hope for delivering God's genuine message of saving faith to those Catholics and ex-Catholics willing to listen is you and me, the Catholic laity. Now, more than ever, there is a need for all of us to pursue holiness and sainthood, becoming missionaries for Christ. Let us give some serious consideration to reverting to the practices in the early days of Christianity, of sharing our resources while encouraging each other in faith and devotion.

PART TWO
CONCLUSION

"I have spread out my hands all day long to a rebellious people, who walk in the way which is not good, following their own thoughts. A people who continue to provoke Me to My Face...."
                              Isaiah 65:2-3

Understandably, a large percentage of present-day Catholics reading this book will have a much different view and experience of the faith than I do. The number of you that were 'grounded' in Catholicism in the same manner that I was during the late 1950s and 1960s is dwindling rapidly. For some readers that are perhaps contemplating a change to a different Church, remaining a Catholic could present a tough decision. It is my firm belief that for some of you, moving away from Catholicism to a different Christian denomination could be a viable option in the pursuit of establishing a clearer and closer relationship with God, which is the ultimate focus and goal of these writings. We should not take lightly and make a decision of this magnitude without a high degree of vetting and discernment. Be sure with any new church you may consider that they based their message and doctrines in Scripture and preach the dogma of salvation by faith.

In today's culture incorporating the broad reach of social media, there are so many opportunities for the Catholic/Christian laity to become involved in evangelization. Hoping to take advantage of this, it is my prayer that this book and the accompanying internet and social media venues (www.voicesoflaity.org) will encourage those who may have abandoned or drifted from their faith to renew and grow their relationship with God, Jesus Christ, the Holy Spirit, and his Church. God's immense blessings are sitting there just waiting for us to claim. For those of you, like me, that remain dedicated to the Catholic faithful, I am confident that these pages will help you reach an even higher level of spiritual fulfillment.

Paul wrote in the Book of Romans about the importance of not only sharing our faith but receiving encouragement from others (Rom 1:12). We know God can speak to and inspire us in countless ways through many sources *if we will take the time to listen*. Sharing our views and testimony regarding our relationships with God and His wonderful blessings is a great way to enhance the inspiration and guidance we get from our clergy and Church leaders. I feel as Catholics; it is something we need to do more of.

At age 68, I have experienced both the 'old school' (pre-Vatican II) and the 'new order' (post-Vatican II) of our faith. At various stages in my life, I have served the Church in almost every capacity that is available to the layperson. Despite this dedication to Church ministries, I still count myself among the worst of sinners. The enemy of sin is repentance and through repentance, I came to realize the abundance of God's forgiveness, grace, and blessings. Being subjected to many of the same temptations and life experiences, writing from the perspective of a lay Catholic I hope provides a different but clearer view than what you might read from something written by a member of the elite media, clergy, or the story of a saint.

PART THREE
THOUGHTS AND PRAYERS

This last section of the book provides my viewpoints on some aspects of Catholic doctrine and how the Catholic faith has affected my life, as well as discussions on key moral issues and dilemmas confronting all of us today. I don't expect you to agree with all, or any, of the following assessments, nor do I believe they are necessarily correct evaluations. They just represent the beliefs ingrained in my heart by the Holy Spirit over many years of prayer and the study of God's Word. Similar to the commentary you would read in a Life Application or Study Bible, please consider these opinions as just 'food for thought.' Most of what I have written, I believe, is grounded in the Word of God, and I hope you will take this into account when formulating your judgments.

After reading this section, I'm sure some of you will classify me as a heretic, 'Cafeteria Catholic,' 'homophobic,' or perhaps a traitor. Know that regardless of what you may think, I extend my love and appreciation to all who have taken the time to read this book. If you would, please take a moment to visit our website www.voicesoflaity.org, here you will find ample opportunity to express your opinions, share your own stories of spiritual discovery, and access many resources that may help steer you on your faith journey. May the love of God the Father and the power of the

Holy Spirit encompass all of you, and let all praise be to Our Lord and Savior Jesus Christ. Amen.

THE SACRAMENTS

Raised in the Catholic faith, I received the sacraments in the order intended. Attending Catholic grammar school and being an altar boy certainly gave me 'a leg up' on my public school friends in experiencing my religion. In third grade, after being 'ordained' as an altar boy, I was convinced the priesthood would be my destiny. Even to the point of celebrating pretend Mass (in Latin) at home using a small cardboard box as the Tabernacle. Tracing the rim of a drinking glass, I'd cut out the center of a 'packed down' slice of Wonder Bread™ to use as the host. Grape juice was perfect for the wine. I would light a few candles, and read the Latin Mass prayers from my St. Joseph's missal. Oh, and let's not forget colored bath towels as vestments. There was nobody that was more 'all in' as a Catholic than I was at 8-9 years old.

Let me first say that I do not think there is anything 'wrong' with receiving any of the Catholic sacraments, and I certainly would discourage no one from doing so. For me, the issues lie with the timing and biblical foundation related to some of the Sacraments. Looking back as an adult on the sacraments of initiation received in my youth, I came to realize they had very little impact on my spiritual development as a Christian and in receiving the genuine message of salvation. Let's look at these Sacraments individually.

Baptism

Do you remember your baptism? If you are a Catholic, you may have seen pictures, but the answer is most likely 'no.' Parents and god-parents presenting a baby, typically under the age of 1, to be baptized in water and oil is a wonderful gesture of having that child welcomed into the faith and God's family. It requires a verbal commitment from the parents and god-parents that the child be raised in the faith, but for obvious reasons, it required no commitment from the one being baptized. Because of the delivery of this sacrament at such a young age, we can argue that it doesn't have much of a direct impact on our spiritual development, but I understand the indirect influence of receiving the sacrament.

If I could make a recommendation to the Church hierarchy, I might suggest having a second 'Baptism of the Spirit,' where Catholics after an intense supervised period of studying Scripture and Catholic doctrine would come forward voluntarily to be baptized again in water and spirit giving themselves to Christ (Rom 6: 3-7). In the early Church, you had to qualify to be baptized by going through an intense period of catechesis indoctrination.

Did you know St. Augustine was not baptized until he was 33 years old? The Roman Emperor Constantine, who in the 4th century was given much credit for temporarily ending the persecution of Christians and legitimizing the Church in Rome was not baptized until he was on his deathbed Why, because while endorsing Christianity he was also head (Pontifus Maximus) of the pagan church in Rome. In merging the two religions, articles like vestments, statues, beads, etc. were introduced into the Catholic religion.

Would it be of greater spiritual benefit if Catholics of any age of 12 or over could present themselves as candidates for organized spiritual education and indoctrination? The sacrament would be given once every 3 months or so. It would be like a 'Holy Orders' for the laity. Your reaction might be 'That is what Confirmation is for,' and we'll address that viewpoint later on.

Penance/Reconciliation

This is a sacrament that I have never understood, even in my youth. As a Catholic school student, we went to confession as a class frequently. I can still recite the traditional 'Act of Contrition' by heart, ingrained in my soul and a wonderful prayer. The sins of our youth were mostly 'minor.' "I lied 3 times, disobeyed my parents twice, I stole once...." After dictating our sins and reciting the Act of Contrition, the priest assigned recitation of several Hail Mary and/or Our Father prayers as 'penance' while kneeling at the altar rail until finished. Looking back, the penance you received had little to do with real repentance. If one of our classmates spent a particularly long time doing their penance, we would surely subject them to some good-natured ridicule later on.

From what I understand, the biblical reference to the sacrament of Reconciliation is John 20:23. 'Whose sins you shall forgive, they are forgiven....'

This, in my opinion, is a loosely connected tie to the scripture compared to the relevance and formal doctrine of the Sacrament set forth by the Church. While some may find relief from the burdens of sin and spiritual comfort in confessing their sins to a priest or even a fellow Catholic, I cannot find anything in the Bible that mandates this is a requirement for salvation. St. Paul, in all his letters, while suggesting we assist each other in overcoming sinful habits, does not suggest that God forgives our sins only through the confession to and blessing of a priest or church elder. Again, I would discourage no one who enjoys the spiritual benefits of priestly confession from continuing to receive the sacrament.

As human beings, we need not look much past the first commandment every day to realize we are in a constant state of sin. This realization dictates that our lives should reside in a perpetual state of discernment, repentance, and reconciliation to God, Our Father, through His Son Jesus Christ. For me, there is no higher standard than this for the forgiveness of sins and acceptance of God's mercy. Maybe I'm alone on this, but I certainly do not know of any person who is in a complete and constant 'state of grace.' Can anyone say they are living without sin?

My guess is that if you were to survey those receiving communion at Mass on any Sunday and ask if they had been to confession in the last year, less than 20% would answer 'yes.' According to Catholic doctrine, the 80% + that have not been to confession are committing a mortal sin by receiving the Eucharist outside a state of grace. It still to this day is difficult for me to understand the biblical logic behind this sacrament.

Holy Eucharist

Of all the sacraments instituted by the Church, this is the one that has had the greatest spiritual impact on me. Receiving the Body and Blood of Our Lord Jesus Christ through the Eucharist is a powerful, spiritually moving event. The best part of this sacrament is we have an opportunity to witness and partake in this wonderful remembrance, miracle, and blessing from Heaven every day during the celebration of the Mass. If for no other reason, this should be the motivating factor for attending Mass at least every Sunday.

Another form of the Eucharist that holds a special place in my heart is the Adoration of the Blessed Sacrament. Our church currently has a newly built and consecrated 24/7 (pre-COVID) adoration chapel. Even with the pandemic going on, my wife and I each take one separate hour on Saturdays. Some of my greatest moments of inspiration from the Holy Spirit have come during that special hour alone with the Body of Christ.

Some Protestant denominations condemn the 'sacrifice of the Mass,' insisting that there is no need to continually 'celebrate' the crucifixion. My view is the Mass is more of a remembrance, carrying on a tradition initiated by Jesus at the Last Supper.

Confirmation

This is one sacrament that I am very familiar with having taught 8th Grade CCD Confirmation classes for over 10 years in the late 1980s and 1990s. While I did my best to teach this age group about the Catholic Faith, the Bible, salvation, and the gifts of the Holy Spirit, the message mostly went 'right over their heads.' If even 5% of my students fully grasped the concept of the spiritual commitment to the faith, they should make with this sacrament, I would have been amazed.

Those students whose parents regularly attended Mass and provided some spiritual guidance and support received a much better feel for the purpose of the sacrament. But again, these students were in a small minority. Every year, about halfway through the program, I would survey the class on how many went to Mass on Sunday. As you might expect, the average was around 25%. Many families, even back then, sent their children through the Confirmation program mostly to fulfill the same tradition theirs and previous generations went through and not out of any real spiritual conviction to commit them to the faith.

Thinking back to my Confirmation, I remember little. Even as a Catholic school kid and altar boy, there was little to no real spiritual impact on me from the sacrament. Much like Baptism, how much more significantly influential and powerful would Confirmation have been if I received it in my twenties or thirties voluntarily, rather than just being 'pushed through' the system at such a young age?

My opinion is this final sacrament of initiation should be voluntary (not forced on a child) and exercised, for most, at a later age. To me, it is one of the primary causes of why we lose so many Catholics as they progress into their late teens and early twenties. Yes, I was one casualty of this process. Hanging on by a thread in the early 1970s, I turned into a Christmas/Easter Catholic, eventually getting married in the Church at age 21. Ironically, it was the teachings of Protestant ministers and my study of the Bible that brought me to my real 'confirmation' and baptism of the Spirit reconnecting me with God, who then subsequently immersed me back into the Catholic Church.

Matrimony, Holy Orders, and Anointing of the Sick

These three are, mostly, 'onetime' sacraments suited to their spiritual purpose.

THE BLESSED VIRGIN MARY

It was October 1962 and our country's fate hinged on the outcome of the Cuban missile crisis. We were on the brink of a nuclear war with Russia, who was trying to get nuclear missiles to launch sites already built in Cuba. This would make for easy targeting and short striking distances to populace areas of the US. President Kennedy put a naval blockade around Cuba to prevent the missiles from being delivered and a showdown with the Soviet Union's Premier, Nikita Khrushchev, became inevitable.

In the course of our daily routine at school in the 4th grade, we would pray at least one decade of the Rosary. On this one day in the middle of the crisis, after learning how to take cover 'under our desks' in the event of an attack (like that was going to help), we spent the entire afternoon session praying the Rosary (kneeling on a wood floor I might add). The crisis was eventually averted as the Soviet Premier backed down, turning the ships back to Russia. We were told the next day by the nuns that our prayers to Mary (not Jesus) saved the day.

The Blessed Virgin Mary (BVM) gave birth to the human nature of Our Lord Jesus Christ. St. John's gospel tells us that the divine nature of Jesus existed from the beginning of time (John 1:1-5). Mary is considered by many the 'Ark of the Covenant' of the New Testament, having carried the

'Word of God' within her. Her faithfulness and devotion to the will of God warrants every honor and praise bestowed upon her.

The practice of praying the rosary and/or directing our prayers to the BVM is prevalent in the Church today, especially among older parishioners. It is a tradition strongly encouraged toward most of the recent generations of Catholics. My question is: Is it beneficial or expedient for us to offer our prayers to the BVM? Is there anything in the Scriptures that would lead us to believe Mary is omnipotent, omniscient, omnipresent, and/or appointed to be a mediator in delivering our prayers to God Our Father in Heaven? If there are thousands of the faithful from around the world praying to Mary at the same time, does she absorb and recognize all of their prayers? Is she continuously delivering our prayers to Jesus so that He can then deliver them to the Father? This is something hard to comprehend, thinking why God would want us to pray this way. It was only about 500 years ago that these customs became firmly established in the Church and eventually grew in popularity as the years went on. During the first 800 years of Christianity, Church history records prayers directed almost exclusively to the Trinity of God.

Praying often for guidance on whether we, as Catholics, should direct any of our prayers **to the BVM**, the Holy Spirit's answer to my heart is always a resounding 'No.' The Spirit tells me there are no prayers that we may choose to guide toward the BVM that we can't target directly to God the Father. God wants us to give Him the praise and glory, our unconditional love, and ask Him for those things that will help us grow spiritually closer to Him. Asking Mary to 'intervene' for us can be a wasted step and distract us from the way Jesus taught us to pray. Our prayers, especially in today's times, need to focus on God, Our Father, imploring Him to send out His Spirit and evangelize the hundreds of thousands of Catholics that have strayed from the faith into repentance. We need to pray to the Holy Spirit for the wisdom and courage to share the Gospel of salvation by faith, a truth that has escaped the comprehension and understanding of so many Catholics. No matter how many rosaries we may pray, the BVM will not appear and save our country, our world, and/or the Catholic Church from God's impending judgments.

This is not an effort on my part to discredit or undervalue the importance of the BVM in God's plan for our salvation, but let us consider the following as it relates to Scripture.

When the disciples asked Jesus to teach them to pray, he instructed them that to be effective, our prayers should be offered directly to the Father in Heaven, giving us the 'Our Father' (Matt 6: 7-13). We should feel the same about praying to the resurrected Jesus and the Holy Spirit. They being one with the Father and comprising the Holy Trinity, but we cannot say the same for the BVM. The first thing He mentioned in answering the question of His disciples was we should pray with sincerity and have a 'conversation' with the Father and not to use 'repetitions' or chants like the pagans do (verse 7). The Gospels show that Jesus always prayed directly to the Father.

Christ is our one mediator with God the Father when it comes to **our salvation** (1 Tim 2:5). Scripture does not tell us we require a mediator when praying to the Father and encourages us to bring all that we have before Him alone. Phil 4: 6-7; 1 John 5:14; Rom 8: 26-27

There are only brief mentions of Mary in the Scriptures once Jesus begins His ministry, including a few historical references in the Gospels and the Acts. At the first recorded miracle of Cana, where Jesus turned the water into wine, Jesus was abrupt with His Mother regarding her request (John 2:4). Showing He needed to separate His human and divine natures, Jesus also exhibited a similar posture later in the Gospel when approached by His disciples while preaching to the crowds and told His mother and brothers were waiting outside and wanted to speak with Him (Matt 12: 46-50). Surely, Jesus was not intentionally 'dismissing' His mother and we can be certain He loved, obeyed, and respected His earthly mother, as God commands all of us to do with our parents. Looking further into the Scriptures, even St.

John, who Jesus told to 'take Mary in' after the crucifixion (John 19: 26-27), makes no mention of her in his writings.

When questioning Catholics on why they pray to Mary and if they worship her, we often hear the argument that they 'venerate' Mary and do not worship her. Given the fine line in the definitions between these two terms, I'm not sure many who pray almost exclusively to the BVM know the difference. Sometimes, as I am in my hour of Adoration of the Blessed Sacrament, I will observe in great disbelief others in the chapel praying the rosary. In our chapel above the altar on the wall, you are facing the Body of Christ crucified on the cross. Sitting on the altar is the Eucharist, symbolizing the Body of Christ displayed in the monstrance. Instead of focusing on Christ, they are praying to the BVM. I really need help in understanding this.

So what about all the appearances by the BVM and documented miracles performed? We should be reminded again of what St. Paul tells us in 2nd Corinthians (2 Cor 11:14) that Satan can present himself as an 'angel of light' and will perform great works to draw our focus away from God and the genuine message of Christ. For this reason, the Church is always tentative to confirm apparitions or visions of Jesus and Mary to people on earth, even if accompanied by what appear to be miracles.

Some on the far Christian Right would say that praying to Mary is Satanic and those that do so are damned to Hell. Certainly, this is not my point of view, but only God will be the judge of how we pray. I contend that most Catholics praying to Mary are doing so with the best of intentions and through their upbringing in the faith, believe they are doing a good thing. My advice is their prayers can be more effective if offered directly to God, Our Father, or through Jesus and the Holy Spirit.

Where did all this attention to Mary start? According to Wikipedia, Marian devotion originated in the 3rd and 4th centuries, propagated by a small sect of the Catholic faith, slowly advancing in stature right into the 15th century. It was only during the late 1400s and 1500s that the Rosary, as we know of it today, came to be.

This was probably the most difficult opinion I have had to express in this book and the part I expect to get the most 'pushback' on.

PURGATORY

This is another of the Church's doctrines that is loosely based on Scripture. It has been a long-time source of revenue for the Church, with issuing indulgences, prayers, and Masses offered for the dead accompanied usually with some kind of monetary payment. The concept of purgatory in Catholicism originated in the 12th century and was developed further in the 1400s and 1500s, around the same time that the rosary and Marian devotion came to the forefront of the Catholic faith. Both these doctrines concerning the BVM and Purgatory were doctrinal challenges posed in the Protestant reformation. The Church's stance on Purgatory also stood in the way of a reunification with the Eastern Orthodox Church at the Second Council of Lyon in 1247 (Source: Wikipedia).

The Church, in its effort to provide scriptural backup to the existence of Purgatory, will site 2 Maccabees 12:43-46 and 1 Corinthians 3:10-15. First, I can tell you that the **Books of Maccabees are not contained in the Hebrew Bible and are only in the 'Catholic Bible.'** If you have a 'standard' Bible, you will not find these books in there. The last line of the 2 Maccabees' scripture is: "It is, therefore, a holy and wholesome thought to pray for the dead, that they may be loosed from sins." In the verses noted from 1st Corinthians, Paul compares our saving faith in Jesus Christ to constructing the foundation of our 'spiritual' building. As we build upon this foundation with our works and deeds, some will be like 'gold, silver, and precious stones,' while others like 'wood, hay, and straw.' God will test these 'building materials' with fire on His judgment day. In verses 14 & 15 Paul tells us that what remains after the test by fire will determine our eternal rewards. Though we may suffer some loss in this judgment, our salvation is secure regardless of our good and bad deeds because we have built our foundation on saving faith in Jesus.

It seems to be quite a leap to discern based on the above scripture verses that there is an additional spiritual realm outside of Heaven and Hell in the afterlife.

As mentioned previously in the chapter on Judgement, Jesus clarified that there is a hierarchy of both eternal punishments and rewards. This made obvious with the quote 'so the last shall be first and the first last' (Matt 20:16). He also mentions in Matthew (Matt 11:22-24) that the eternal punishment for some will be 'more tolerable' than for others. These quotes of Jesus confirm the basis of our judgement and eternal reward or punishment are evaluated according first to our faith, love, devotion, and obedience to God and then the extent to which we have loved our neighbors. It is hard to dispute these words of Jesus telling us we will not all experience Heaven or Hell to the same degree.

Did Jesus descend into 'Abraham's Bosom' to bring the Old Testament saints with Him to Heaven after the crucifixion? I believe He did, but my understanding is this was a onetime event. If there were such a place as Purgatory, wouldn't Jesus have brought this up and emphasized a need for us to pray for those who have gone before us to end their suffering or 'purification?' The Catholic Church came up with a system of 'indulgences' that goes into effect if you pray certain prayers or follow specific guidelines. If you search the Internet or review the catechism for the term 'indulgences,' you'll see a myriad of rules and regulations for both plenary and partial indulgences. A plenary indulgence shoots a soul directly from Purgatory up to Heaven, removing all suffering, while a 'partial' just removes some sufferings. Were these systems of indulgences and their requirements divinely inspired? Or are they just an arbitrary set of rules? Reading through these indulgence requirements, I ask myself, where and when did they come up with this? Doesn't this portray a sense of arrogance in making our own rules dictating to God when an individual can enter Heaven from Purgatory?

If Purgatory cleanses/purifies our souls before allowed to enter Heaven, then how can it be that a plenary indulgence executed by a living being on earth wipes a soul completely clean while faith in the shed Blood of Jesus at the Cross does not? For me, the notion that there is a payment to be made for our sins by our own sufferings after death diminishes the ultimate atonement of the saving Blood of Jesus on the cross. If you could somehow tell St. Paul that the sacrifice made by Jesus on the cross was insufficient to get us to Heaven and that additional (temporal) suffering individually after death according to our deeds would be required, I believe you would be in for a long sermon.

It is interesting to see the doctrines of the Church that do not have a firm foundation in Scripture are becoming almost obscure in the Church today. Outside of maybe a few 'old-timers', like myself, you hear little about praying for the souls in Purgatory. Perhaps in November on 'All Souls Day,' you might hear a mention. Receiving the sacrament of Penance/Reconciliation is a rapidly disappearing occurrence. Could there be a Purgatory? As Bishop Barron says about the existence of Hell: 'We have to consider the possibility it exists.' If there is no Purgatory, then 'praying for the dead' is a wasted effort. The souls of the departed are in Paradise or Hell, waiting for the final judgment. Nothing we do here on earth can change their eternal fate. Let us focus then our prayers and evangelization on the living, encouraging all to deepen and strengthen their relationship to God while they can.

In finishing this topic, I will reveal that I recite the words "My Lord and My God" at the elevation of the Eucharist and the chalice at the consecration for each Mass I attend, just in case. This small prayer results in a partial indulgence worth only 7 years and 7 quarantines (whatever that is?), but it may just help someone out. For those of you that attend daily Mass, according to the Church, if you do this for one straight week, it equals a plenary indulgence. My son, a former seminarian and devoted Catholic, assured me he would exercise a plenary indulgence for me after my death. So I guess I'm covered? Yes, I'm covered by the Blood of my Lord and Master Jesus Christ.

ABORTION

One of the most contested issues in our society today is the practice of legalizing abortion. The center of the debate for many hinges on exactly when 'life begins' for an unborn fetus. Most of the doctrines related to Christian churches, including Catholicism, will tend to agree that life begins at conception. While others may take the view that life does not begin until there is a detectable heartbeat, and others not until physical birth. Pro-choice advocates argue that women should have the choice to do as they please with their bodies, supporting abortions under the guise of 'women's health,' giving no consideration to the life and health of the unique 'body' living inside them.

Did you know that in a 2019 'Pew Research' survey, it shows 56% of Catholics believe that abortion should be legal in all/most cases (Fahmy, 2020)?

No matter where you might stand on this issue, the question we, as Catholics and Christians, need to ask is what is God's point of view? If we take a step back and consider the theory that God agrees with the principle of life beginning at conception, wouldn't it then consequently support the notion that destroying an unborn baby in the mother's womb would be considered an act of murder? In the Old Testament, we see God speak to His prophets regarding His great displeasure for this sin that often occurred during acts of war by invading armies (Amos 1:13; 2 Kings 8:12; 2 Kings

15:16; Hosea 13:16). If it is God's will that all pregnancies should be carried to their full term, then the millions of abortions performed around the world over the past 50 years would be (and continue to be) by far the largest genocide in human history.

Based on this conviction, I struggle to imagine the horrendous punishment God has in store for those politicians and judges that have created and supported laws legalizing this act. Surely those identifying themselves as Catholics or Christians engaging in the legitimizing of abortions have been acting absent of the fear of God. For those mothers, some encouraged and supported by the child's father, that underwent these procedures and do not repent, will the financial or social benefit they gained from procuring an abortion outweigh the penalty they will receive in eternal punishment?

The statistics regarding abortion are staggering. According to Guttmacher™ and Johnston Archives ™ in 1963, there were 390 reported abortions in the US, but from 1975 through 2008 there were over one million reported abortions per year in our country alone after the Roe v Wade decision in 1973. In recent years there has been a modest decline with the numbers falling below 1 million per year. The percentage of abortions performed because of rape, incest, and jeopardy to the mother's health combined are far less than 10% of the total, revealing the vast majority of abortions performed strictly as a method of birth control. Reasons given mostly include financial hardship, social disadvantage, and lack of an established relationship with the father.

We need to remember that God has given us a free will and is by nature 'pro-choice.' What escapes so many is there will be consequences, both good and bad, depending on those 'choices' we make. You may 'get away with murder' right now, but know there will eventually be an extreme and eternal price to pay.

We see in the Scriptures examples of judgment from God that can be levied not only on individuals but from a societal perspective as well. A practice going on in Israel during the time of Jeremiah the prophet (around 580

BC), comparable with the abortion crisis of today, was the sacrificing of young male Jewish children by burning them to death at the altar of the gods Moloch and Baal. God told Jeremiah that His people have 'filled this place with the blood of the innocents' (Jer 19: 4-6). As mentioned earlier in this book, the attitude of the Jews in those days was 'they were doing nothing wrong' (Jer 2: 34-35). This same lack of remorse exists in our western societies today. God built up Israel and Judah to be great nations during the reigns of King David and King Solomon, much as He did to the Western nations after World War II. In its affluence, the Jewish people turned from God and began worshiping Baal and other idols, eventually leading to God's utter destruction of Judah, Israel, and even His holy city of Jerusalem by King Nebuchadnezzar. Are there lessons to be learned here regarding God's impending judgment on the world today?

Some may inquire if it is possible to repent from the sin of abortion? Of course, it is, the suffering and death of Jesus on the cross were for all the sins of those that put faith in His redemption. God accepts repentance through a person's direct relationship with Him. Outward expressions of repentance could come as support for pro-life groups, and perhaps counseling of young women who are considering abortions.

We as Christians must, at all costs, openly display our love and support to both those that previously have had, or are even now considering, an abortion. Like with everything else, there should be no room in the Christian heart for hate, judgment, or disparagement toward anyone. Always remember, God is the ultimate judge and will serve His justice to those that He deems to have lived absent of faith and outside of His will. We must strive to make our voices heard to rid our society of this evil practice and persevere in the call to repentance.

SEXUAL SIN

The term 'sexual sin' can now probably be defined as an oxymoron, having become, mostly, obsolete. Except for a small percentage of our population, sexual activity outside of marriage and sin are now mutually exclusive conditions. After all, we have the choice to do with our bodies as we please. The only sexual activities that have maintained some level of accountability are sexual relations outside of a relationship with joined sexual partners and adultery for married couples. Touching on this topic in Part II of this book, we looked at the impact sexual sin has had on the leadership of our Church. Here, we will take a broader look at the influence this phenomenon has had on our societies.

If you were born after 1970, you grew up in an age of sexual freedom. The ideologies and practices related to sex in the generations that preceded this era are but ancient history to these cohorts. Both the general and social media over the past 50 years have glorified sex to the extent that one's sexual prowess can be worn as a badge of honor among peers, while sexual purity often carries with it ridicule and scorn. Television, movies, music, social media, the internet, and the pornographic industry are all venues that have shaped our mindsets and beliefs, contributing greatly to how we perceive our sexual 'freedoms' today. Actions without consequence and freedom without responsibility have led to surges in sexually transmitted diseases and abortions. Much like we discussed with abortion, it is our duty and responsibility to seek the will of God as it pertains to these matters. As the 'Baby Boomers', the last remaining generation to have witnessed the sexual norms of the past die off, who will be left to pursue the true will of God related to sexual matters?

There are numerous instances in the Bible where God has executed His judgment on individuals and societies engaged in blatant sexual immorality. One example we've mentioned before is God's destruction of Judah, Israel, and Jerusalem and the enslavement of His Chosen People to Babylon. The annihilation of Sodom and Gomorrah is probably the most famous of these episodes and the one most familiar to you (Genesis, Chap. 18 & 19). In this biblical story, we see that even God's servant Lot's two daughters, saved from His devastation of these cities, were heavily influenced by the immoralities of their society. So much so they plotted to have incestuous relationships with their father, after getting him drunk. As detailed in Chapter 19 of Genesis, they both bore sons from those encounters that would later become bitter enemies of Israel (Moab & Ben-ammi (father of Ammons)).

Looking further into the scriptures, including Jesus's teachings, we realize God's true intent regarding sexual relationships. God's plan from the beginning was that once you established a sexual relationship with your partner, there should be a corresponding commitment to this person for life. God hated the sin of sexual immorality so much that in the days of the Old Testament, the established punishment for those caught in adultery was death by stoning. In the New Testament St. Paul tells us, God, out of His disdain for the sin, 'gave them over' or gave up on them to let them do as they please, not just for the sexual sin but for the influence that sexual impurity had on their whole lives and demeanors (Rom 1:24-27) Many New Testament Bible verses related to sexual morality can be found by searching on the internet, and below are just a few to get you started.

1 Cor 6:9-10, 18
2 Cor 12:21
Eph 5:5
Heb 13:4
1 Thes 4:3-5

Matt 5:28-32

Aside from evaluating the influences levied on our spirit from these grave sins committed against God, we can also contemplate the many negative effects on our social and economic systems. According to the census bureau (US Census Bureau, 2021) in 1961, around 10% of family households were headed by single-parent women, and by 2015 that number had almost doubled to over 19%. These single mothers often have to work multiple jobs just to keep their families afloat, having to leave their children with relatives, daycare providers, or, even worse, to fend for themselves. Fathers abandon their families for many reasons and the results of fatherless families often lead to welfare dependency, crime, and/or financial ruin for their former partners and children. There is a comprehensive article on this subject I encourage you to read by *'Marripedia.org'* that has extensive commentary, data, and references (Marripedia, 2020).

For those of you that may struggle with the demons of sexual sin, I can tell you from personal experience that with prayer, the study of God's Word, and perseverance of repentance you can overcome these evil spirits haunting your soul, and harming your spiritual connection to God.

Do I expect there will be a 'revival' and a return to the sexual norms of the past more in line with God's will soon? My guess is that just the opposite will occur. We will continue to see our children and grandchildren moving even further away from the will of the Father in pursuit of self-glory, strongly encouraged and inspired by the globalist political climate and supported by the mass media. Let us pray that Our Lord's second coming will be soon.

DIVORCE

This topic has always intrigued me when considering how God might judge those that have experienced divorce in their lives. When asked about this topic by His disciples, Jesus 'pulled no punches' clarifying that God intends that once a man and woman are joined in marriage, they should remain together for life (Matt 19:8-9; Matt 5:31; Luke 16:18). The only 'out' He gave us was if adultery was involved.

Some questions I ponder on this subject are: Should a woman or a man have to endure a physically or mentally abusive relationship, for the sake of their salvation? Does being bored with each other qualify as a legitimate excuse for divorce? How do couples once deeply in love and willing to make a commitment to each other for life through marriage grow so far apart or suddenly become incompatible? Is it selfishness by one or both of the partners that leads to this outcome? Who is ultimately responsible for the impact of divorce on children? Do couples even consider what God's response will be to their divorce? Based on the teaching of Jesus, does God consider sexual relations outside of the marriage after divorce or a second or third marriage to be adultery? If you become divorced, why not redirect your focus toward devoting your life to a renewed commitment to God?

The answers to the questions above are ones that can be debated among the many Christian denominations out there. The Catholic faith, to its credit, has taken a pretty firm stand on divorce, especially for those marriages between baptized Catholics where the ceremony was performed in a Catholic Church. The Catechism of the Church explains its position on divorce. A great article written for *'Catholic.com' by Leila Miller* gives us eight key points to know regarding the Church's position on divorce, including direct links to catechism references (Miller, 2017).

Some would say as Christ bore His suffering on the cross for us, we too should bear the sufferings that may arise in the marriage relationship for the sake of committing to God's will in keeping a marriage together for life. Can we say the pain and negatives of 'staying together' are greater than those we can tolerate by being apart? The argument would be that most any suffering we may endure from a personal relationship would pale compared to the pain of Christ's suffering and death.

I have received no greater blessing from God than the day he delivered into my life my amazing wife who has put up with me for the last 47 years. For those past, present, and future that have or will have faced the difficulties of separation and/or divorce, I pray for you and encourage you to pray to the Father for guidance and comfort through the Holy Spirit.

TITHING

We can be relatively brief on this topic, as the concept is pretty simple. God bestows His blessings on us every day, giving us our health, wealth, food on the table, a proper place to sleep, etc. Since the beginning of humanity, God has required us to make a 'sacrifice' by offering a portion of what He has given us back to Him and those that are less fortunate than we are. One of the very first Bible stories, Cain killing his brother Able, related to acceptable vs. unacceptable sacrifices offered to God (Genesis Chapter 4).

Probably the most common misconception most people have when it comes to our earthly possessions is that they belong to us. Instead of basking in our own glory, we need to realize and come to accept the principle that all we have, our houses, cars, boats, money, retirement funds, etc., have been given to us through God's blessings and could, if it is His will, be taken from us just as easily.

The word 'tithe' is derived from an old English word, which means one-tenth. We often hear this word in Scripture, especially in the Old Testament, as it relates to the **minimum** of what God asks us to 'give back' from His bountiful blessings. To keep the math easy, let's say that your family income is $1,000/week. This means that your weekly tithe should be a minimum of $100/week. This does not mean they should disperse this amount exclusively to support parishes and congregations. Giving to charities, the sick, the poor, the homeless, etc. would also fall under the 'tithe umbrella.' Can you just imagine what the world would be like if everyone followed God's direction and gave a tithe to support Christ's message of salvation through His Christian Churches and to help the poor and downtrodden? In addition, having the ability to distribute these offerings fairly to those in need, absent of any embezzlement or corruption. This is a great example of how much better off the world would be if we all acted according to God's instructions and plan.

Remembering my days as a young Catholic, our family would receive a stack of dated envelopes for the weekly offerings to be put in the basket at Sunday Mass. They expected the children to put a quarter in their envelope and the adults at least a dollar or two. This was back in the early to mid-1960s. If you observe the offerings now being made by the faithful as the basket goes around, still a good percentage only contribute a dollar or two. In case you haven't noticed, running a parish is a lot more expensive than it was in the 1960s. It is certainly not my business to judge anyone on what they give to the Church, but they should know that according to the Scriptures, God will judge and bless them according to what they give.

I'll finish this off with a short testimony of how God has blessed me and my family financially. Yes, I too was one of those who would just throw a single dollar in the offertory basket when it came around to show those around me I was giving something and not 'stiffing' the Church. It never occurred to me that this was really not a 'sacrifice' or an offering even remotely considered as being pleasing to God. As you might expect, living outside of His will and without God's blessings, my family was struggling financially, even to the point of bankruptcy. This is an example of how God got my attention. It was only through my 'spiritual awakening' and reading of the Scriptures that I came to realize how I had come to 'rob God' of what He asks for and deserved, and how I needed to make amends by giving so much more of my time, talent, and treasure to Him. Needless to say, once I gave God His just due, even though it was difficult at that time, His financial blessings slowly, over several years, poured out on my family leading us to a newfound humility and prosperity.

It is easy to find testimony from the many who have experienced financial blessings once they embraced a loving and giving tithing spirit according to God's will. What would be challenging is finding examples of those whose financial situation worsened as they gave more of their time, treasure, and talent.

There are numerous Scripture verses related to tithing and giving and I've put some below for you to reference. My favorite is from **Malachi 3: 8-10**. Here, God talks of cursing the nation for 'robbing Him.' The people complain they don't understand why He accuses them and how they are robbing Him? He challenges them to 'put Him to the test' and bring their tithings as they should. Then they will see how He delivers on his promises to send His blessings 'until there is no more need.' Further references:

Lev 27:30 2 Cor 9:7; Luke 6:38; Prov 11:34; Mark 12:41-44

SALVATION BY FAITH

By now, you may be sick of hearing the mention of the phrase describing this last topic, an expression brought up repeatedly throughout the book. The reason behind making so much of an effort to stress this subject is my concern that so many Catholics and Christians, like I did, missed this vital message so critically important to our eternal destiny. Like many of us raised in the Catholic faith, the Church led me to believe 'being good' would get me into heaven. Pray, follow the commandments, be good to others, and be engaged in Catholic traditions were taught as the main protocols we must adhere to in order to gain eternal reward. While all these actions are commendable, Scripture tells us they have little to do with our salvation.

Moving through the Catholic education system from 1st through the 9th grades reinforced these suggested practices, deep-seating them into my soul. At no point in my life, even for several years when I morphed into a Christmas/Easter Catholic, did I ever have a concern for my eternal fate. I was a kind, 'good person' raising a family, going to church once in a while, having fun in life, and not 'hurting anyone.' Surely, if something had happened to me and I were to pass away, God would not 'send me' to Hell. I would still go to Heaven. After all, my parents baptized me in the Catholic Church. It was only by the grace of God that He brought me to His Word to show me how very wrong I was and how much my eternal fate was in jeopardy. Taking a careful look at the words of Jesus, St. Paul, and other authors of the New Testament, I realized I had been ignoring God and without knowing it becoming more and more separated from Him. Never did I give a thought of how subjected to the distractions of Satan I had become.

Founded in the encouragement of so many Godly preachers, there came a time I finally convinced myself to read the Bible in its entirety. As I've stated before, growing up Catholic, they did not encourage me to read the Bible on my own. It became so clear to me after the first time reading the Word of God from beginning to end that missing from all the spiritual lessons and guidance I received as a Catholic was the most key Christian doctrine of all, 'salvation by faith.' While I may have heard the term briefly mentioned in a reading at Mass or perhaps a sermon or two, never was it explained to the extent that it needed and deserved to be. Subsequent readings and study of the Bible, along with the heartfelt wisdom and heavenly aid from the Holy Spirit, reinforced my belief and understanding of how God reconciles himself to us exclusively through saving faith in His Son.

So, what does the Word of God tell us? Let's review just a few critical points:

Only a few of us will make it to Heaven: Matt 7:13-23; Luke 13:23-28; Isaiah 35:8; Luke 6:46; Matt 22:14.

None of us are 'good,' all fall short and are subject to God's judgment: Rom 3:10; Rom 3:23-25; Rom 5:1-21; 1 John 1:8; Psalm 14:1-3; Psalm 53:1-4.

Our reconciliation to the Father and our salvation is only through our faith in Jesus: Eph 2:8-9; Rom 3:28; John 3:16; Rom 10:9; Heb 11:1-40.

If someone were to ask you 'do you believe in God,' your answer would most likely be 'yes, of course I do.' If asked, 'is your faith based in the redemptive suffering, death, and resurrection of Jesus Christ as payment for your sins, the determining source of your righteousness before God, and your ultimate salvation?' You may scratch your head, trying to understand the question.

Faith is so much more than just saying 'I believe.' True 'saving faith' is not just repeatedly mouthing words, but should be described as a state of action, a perpetual mindset putting us in constant pursuit of the knowledge to understand the will and mind of God. It is the recognition of His plan for our salvation realized through the atoning suffering and death on the cross of His Son Jesus Christ and sharing this message with others. It is a devotion to and cherishing of the Word of God and all the wisdom it contains. Faith is being humble before God, acknowledging we are sinners, submitting ourselves to His will, and repenting from those actions we embrace that offend God. Our commitment to becoming 'slaves' to Our Lord and Master, Jesus Christ, is a giant step toward saving faith.

We must also come to realize all that we have comes from God through His blessings and grace and then share this abundance and joy with others. We can apply these lifestyle commitments as conditions of 'saving faith.' Jesus tells us we could move mountains with genuine faith as small as a mustard seed (Matt 17:20).

The epistle of St. James (James 2:17-24) talks about how our works or deeds extend our saving faith. We can't say we have faith and then go on living our lives contrary to the will of God, or 'hiding in our basements,' holding back on expressing and showing our faith to others through our good works. Yet, our deeds are fleeting with God in the absence of faith. **Probably the two most important things you can take from this book are that our faith in and devotion to God and His Son Jesus Christ will be the sole basis of determining our salvation. Our works, all that we do here on earth, will be judged on the throne of God to determine the level of our eternal reward or punishment.**

Looking around us in the world today, we can envision a time coming very soon when our faith will be tested. There will be persecution around the globe and those saints that persevere and endure in their faith under all circumstances can be assured of being welcomed into the glory of the Kingdom of God. It is my fervent prayer that you will be one of them. Amen!!

Form more on salvation by faith, visit our blog page @ www.voicesoflaity.org/blog.

AMEN!

At last, we come to the end... or is it the beginning? First, I'd like to extend my humble gratitude and appreciation to all who took the time to read through what has been for me a monumental undertaking. Inspired by the Holy Spirit, I did all I could when writing to choose my words carefully. It was not lost on me that the reader's eternal destiny might be 'hanging in the balance.' If through the lessons learned in this book, even one soul comes to saving faith in Jesus Christ and inherits a place in the Kingdom of God, how much more glory and honor will be given to God, Our Father, in Heaven and His Son, Jesus Christ.

At this point, I'd like to reiterate my belief that even though Satan may well have already overtaken the throne of St. Peter in Rome, still many of the Catholic faithful are in a quest for holiness, in search of the truth. Led by Archbishop Viganò, there are many good bishops and priests still out there not afraid to defy and confront, even on local levels, the corrupt leadership that has infiltrated the Church. With the evangelization of God's truths portrayed so vividly in the scriptures, a great void has been left by the clergy in getting the message to us, the Catholic laity. For the shrinking number of Catholics that do still attend Mass each week, the messages we receive are often weak and distorted. So, who is left to do the desperately needed work in the mission fields of Catholics? How can we reach the younger generation of Catholics whose faith in and devotion to God is almost non-existent? The burden seems now to fall squarely on us, the laity.

So what can we do, as laity, to bring God's message to our fellow Catholics and Christians while our faith, the family unit, our democracy, and the fundamental laws of God are under vicious attack by those that would endeavor to destroy these principles? Here are some steps we can follow:

Pray, pray, pray, pray to God, Our Father in Heaven for the clergy, for the poor, for the homeless, for the downtrodden, for the conversion of sinners, for Catholics to open their hearts to receive the true gifts of Wisdom and Understanding from the Holy Spirit.

Work tirelessly to reconcile ourselves and our lifestyle, identifying God's plan and will for us.

Make it a point to actively 'Listen to God' through the reading of Scripture, 'tuning in' to the voice of the Holy Spirit within us, and paying attention to God's involvement in our everyday circumstances.

Come to completely acknowledge and understand God's truth of 'salvation by faith' so that we can confidently profess and explain the concept to others that they may come to accept and embrace this belief.

Evangelize to others we know, our families, especially the younger generations, our fellow parishioners, join Bible studies.

Do not subsidize any clergy (Cardinal/Bishop Appeals) who endorse doctrines you believe are contrary to God's will.

We are here to provide you with continuing assistance in your endeavors if you so choose to follow Christ on a path to sainthood. It is my sincere wish that all who are concerned with the spiritual well-being of current and former Catholics will contribute to and become active followers of the Voices of Catholic Laity (VOCAL) Ministries website. At www.voicesoflaity.com you will find many resources to assist you in answering the 'Last Call to Sainthood' and strengthening your relationship with God.

May the peace of Christ be with you always. Amen!

BIBLIOGRAPHY

Authors, M. (2019, October 3). *100s of accused priests living under radar with no oversight.* Retrieved from Associated Press: https://apnews.com/article/crime-sexual-abuse-by-clergy-sexual-abuse-sexual-assault-the-reckoning-6109dc3f9e744298ae3fd5fe607f0a3c

BBC. (2013, February 12). *Lightning Strikes St. Peter's Basilica as Pope Resigns.* Retrieved from BBC: https://www.bbc.com/news/av/world-europe-21421810

Cahn, J. (2017). *The Paradigm: The Ancient Blueprint That Holds the Mystery of Our Times.* Lake Mary, FL: Frontline Charisma Media.

Fahmy, D. (2020, October 20). *8 key findings about Catholics and abortion.* Retrieved from Pew Research: https://www.pewresearch.org/fact-tank/2020/10/20/8-key-findings-about-catholics-and-abortion/

Francis, P. (2020). *Fratelli Tutti.* Rome: Assocciazione Amici del Papa.

Illinois Regional Bank. (1988). *Life Application Bible.* Wheaton, IL: Tyndale House Publishers.

Jones, J. (2021, May 29). *Church Membership Falls Below Majority for First Time.* Retrieved from Gallup: https://news.gallup.com/poll/341963/church-membership-falls-below-majority-first-time.aspx

Lawler, P. (2018). *The Smoke of Satan.* Charlotte, NC: TAN Books.

Marripedia. (2020). *Effects of Fatherless Families on Crime Rates.* Retrieved from Marripedia: https://marripedia.org/effects_of_fatherless_families_on_crime_rates

Marshall, D. T. (2019). *'Infiltration–The Plot to Destroy the Church from Within'*. Manchester, NH: Crisis Publications.

Martel, F. (2019). *In the Closet of the Vatican: Power, Homosexuality, Hypocrisy*. Rome: Bloomsbury Continuum.

MacArthur, J. (2020). *MacArthur Study Bible*. Nashville, TN: Thomas Nelson.

Meloni, J. (2021). *The St. Gallen Mafia*. Gastonia, NC: TAN Books.

Miller, L. (2017, March 24). *Eight Things You Have To Know About The Church's Teaching On Divorce*. Retrieved from Catholic Answers: https://www.catholic.com/magazine/online-edition/eight-things-you-have-to-know-about-the-churchs-teaching-on-divorce

Neuman, S. (2020, November 10). *Vatican Report Says Pope John Paul II Knew About Allegations Against Former Cardinal*. Retrieved from NPR: https://www.npr.org/2020/11/10/933382721/vatican-report-says-pope-john-paul-ii-knew-about-allegations-against-former-card

Saad, L. (2018, April 9). *Church Attendance Among Catholics Resumes Downward Slide*. Retrieved from Gallup: https://news.gallup.com/poll/232226/church-attendance-among-catholics-resumes-downward-slide.aspx

Stanley, C. (1985). *How To Listen To God*. Nashville, TN: Thomas Nelson.

Stanley, C. (n.d.). *Home*. Retrieved from In Touch Ministries: www.intouch.org.

Thigpen, P. (2019). *'Saints Who Saw Hell and Other Catholic Witnesses to the Fate of the Damned'*. Charlotte, NC: TAN Books.

US Census Bureau. (2021, November). *Historical Households Tables (Table HH1)*. Retrieved from US Census Bureau: https://www.census.gov/data/tables/time-series/demo/families/households.html

Vigano, A. (2018, August). *Vigano Letter.* Retrieved from Wall Street Journal Online: https://online.wsj.com/media/Viganos-letter.pdf

Vigano, A. (2020, October 25). *Archbishop Vigano warns President Trump about 'Great Reset' in an Open Letter.* Retrieved from Catholic Online: https://www.catholic.org/news/national/story.php?id=85039&from=groupmessage

Wolf, A. (2021, February 12). *New York Catholic Diocese Bankruptcies Put Abuse Claims in Limbo.* Retrieved from Bloomberg Law: https://news.bloomberglaw.com/bankruptcy-law/new-york-catholic-diocese-bankruptcies-put-abuse-claims-in-limbo

www.ingramcontent.com/pod-product-compliance
Lightning Source LLC
LaVergne TN
LVHW020933090426
835512LV00020B/3332